MUSICAL GAMES, FINGERPLAYS AND RHYTHMIC ACTIVITIES FOR EARLY CHILDHOOD

Marian Wirth
Verna Stassevitch
Rita Shotwell
Patricia Stemmler

PARKER PUBLISHING COMPANY, INC.
West Nyack, New York

*To our families for their loving support and encouragement, and
to the many teachers and children we have worked with over the
years who shared with us their ideas and enthusiasm for musical
games.*

Illustrations by Pat Stemmler

Library of Congress Cataloging in Publication Data

Main entry under title:
Musical games, fingerplays, and rhythmic activities
    for early childhood.
    Melodies with chord symbols.
    "For classroom teachers"—Introd.
    1. Games with music. 2. Children's songs—
United States. 3. Finger play. I. Wirth, Marian
Jenks.
M1993.M9815   1983   82-22371
ISBN 0-13-607085-X

Printed in the United States of America

About the Authors

Marian Wirth received a Bachelor of Science in Education from Ohio State University and a Master of Arts in Learning Disabilities from St. Louis University. She taught perceptual motor skills at the Miriam School in St. Louis for eight years and was an early childhood education specialist with the Child Day Care Association of St. Louis for four and one half years. She has also taught child development courses at Washington University, St. Louis, and at St. Louis Community College. She has also given numerous workshops for teachers. Presently certified as an educational examiner, Mrs. Wirth is the author of *Teacher's Handbook of Children's Games: A Guide to Developing Perceptual Motor Skills*. This book has been recently published in paperback under the title, *Games for Growing Children*, Parker Publishing Co., Inc., West Nyack, New York.

Verna Stassevitch received Bachelor of Science and Bachelor of Music degrees from Skidmore College. She has pursued further study at the graduate level in Orff-Schulwerk training. She was supervisor of music in Newburyport, Massachusetts for two years, and director of music at The Wilson School for twelve years. She is presently headmistress of The Wilson School (six years) and still finds time to teach music to the upper grades there. She presents many workshops for teachers, and has taught music education classes at Fontbonne College in St. Louis, and St. Louis Community College at Forest Park. She has also served as consultant and instructor in a special program (correlating music and language) at the Miriam School in St. Louis, serving children with learning disabilities. She is a member of the national and local chapters of the National Association for Education of the Young Child, the Elementary Heads Association, the Independent Schools Association of Central States, the Educational Confederation of Metropolitan St. Louis, the National and local chapters of American Orff-Schulwerk Association, and the Music Educators' National Conference.

Rita Shotwell received her Bachelor of Arts in Communications from St. Louis University and is currently working on her Master's degree in Early Childhood Education. She has extensive training in the Orff approach to teaching music and some Kodaly musical training. For the past twelve years, she has been Early Childhood Consultant for Winn (Strub) Music Company and teaches at Hope United Presbyterian Church Nursery School, Shriners' Hospital for Crippled Children, and Arts for Older Adults classes for Cemrel, Inc. She has given many workshops for educators at local, state and national meetings, and received a Certificate of Merit from the St. Louis Suburban Music Educators' Association. She is a member of the local and national Orff-Schulwerk Association, the local and national Association for the Education of Young Children, the Midwest Kodaly Association, and the Dalcroze Society.

Pat Stemmler studied music education at Butler University, and has been teaching music and art to preschool and primary-age children for the last ten years. Currently she is teaching at the Ethical Society Nursery School and Ladue Community School Extended Day Kindergarten in St. Louis, Missouri. She has given many music workshops in the St. Louis area. Illustrating has been her hobby for many years, and she has designed logos for the Coalition for the Environment, the St. Louis Association for the Education of Young Children, and the St. Louis Chapter of the American Orff-Schulwerk Association.

Introduction

The idea for this book resulted from a casual encounter between two of the authors. Both of us had been working with children and teachers for many years, and seemed to have an endless reservoir of ideas. Sharing this reservoir of material seemed very natural, and two other well-known teachers quickly came to mind, and we joined forces. An early Sunday morning meeting date was set, and work progressed slowly but steadily from then on.

We were unanimous in our agreement that the book should be written for classroom teachers. Music and physical education specialists would also find many useful materials in the collection, and families could get a great deal of enjoyment from singing, playing, or chanting these activities together.

We tested directions out on each other. Everything had to be simple, clear, and obvious, and readily adaptable to many different classroom situations. The materials were picked for their time-tested appeal and popularity with hundreds of children. Our aim was to bring together in one volume the favorites of four different, experienced teachers, then present them "ready-packaged" for instant use.

All of the activities involve some kind of action. We all recognize that young children learn in a variety of ways, but we also know that learning is inseparable from movement during the early years. What exactly do children learn from an active musical game that they might not learn from an ordinary song?

Singing with a group requires that each child coordinate his or her voice with that of the group, and be sensitive to the group's speed and tone. But in a song like "Pop! Goes the Weasel," jumping up at the right time requires extra attentiveness, anticipating a signal, and getting the body ready to jump at a precise time. Combining vocal and physical action demands a different kind of thought, along with the coordination of the mind, the voice, and the body. And so, with each activity, a different pattern of response is called for, depending on the directions for the song or game. Before long, the child has many patterns of response tucked away in his or her brain's storage department. Every activity mastered makes the subsequent ones easier. The child builds "game know-how," "musical know-how" and "social know-how."

The most active part of the learning process occurs when the game is new. This is when all "cylinders of thought and muscular control are operating." Coordination has not yet become smooth, but because of the humor and playfulness of the activity, children do not become frustrated. They struggle with great good humor to "get it all together." Besides, because no score is kept, the game is exciting and pleasant, even when at the "stumbling" stage. It is during the "stumbling" stage that most of the learning occurs, including new words, new rhythms, or new ways of moving through a routine. When the game has become familiar and automatic, interest may wane. Then it is time to bring out a new activity. Even if the children do not tire of a familiar musical game, learning begins to drop off, and it is up to the teacher to create a new challenge, either by varying the old game or by moving on to a new one.

Aside from greasing the wheels of thought and expression through coordinating the senses, the body and the mind, all these musical activities and fingergames have a "script"—the words. These words are all in sentence form, some simple, some complex. Aside from their content, which may vary from instructive to whimsical, the words of the song provide a model of complete sentences, careful phrasing, and new meanings. They model English grammar, and may introduce, in the case of the preschoolers, new parts of speech in the most easy and enjoyable way.

Finally, every game or activity contributes to the children's social skills, simply because each is performed in a group, to which each child can be a successful contributor. Many of the games are so easy that each child can perform at his or her natural level, without affecting others in the group. In some activities there is cooperative interaction, so these games may be chosen on the basis of age, or else tried out to see if they "fly." Challenge exists, but without competition, without winning or losing, and without emphasizing the more "successful" children. Many games, once learned, can be played at home or on the playground without the teacher's help. Without exception, each child will add to her or his organizational, expressive and memory skills. By cooperating and following a few simple directions, each will learn how to create a joyful, rich experience out of thin air.

The format of the book is consistent throughout. You can see at a glance the appropriate age levels, the educational benefits and any materials needed. We have also included a detailed table of contents to make the book easy to use. We suggest that you become familiar with each activity yourself, before presenting it to your children—it always makes a difference in the success of the material. Use the pictures as aids, especially to help children in following directions. Pat Stemmler has been very skillful in her illustrations and has selected key elements of each action. Guitar, autoharp and piano chords are notated for all music, and you will notice that most songs have no more than two or three chords, which is characteristic of folk music. Tunes are also notated in a range that is comfortable for both children and adults. Sometimes rhythmic notation has been added to make a spoken activity easier to follow.

You'll find that all the material in this book invites repetition. It also provides a jumping-off point for teachers, from which they can carry the ideas a bit further and add their own special variations.

We, the authors, have enjoyed a great many hours of fun and companionship assembling this book. Now we hope that others will find equal enjoyment in it, and many uses for all the activities.

In no case was a song of known authorship used without credits. The vast majority of songs or chants were taught to us over the years by young children or teachers, usually during a class or workshop. To these old folksongs we have sometimes added original movements. We are grateful to the generations of singers and players who kept alive these songs, some of which go back hundreds of years. Completely original songs or games have been labelled with the name of one of the four authors.

Rita Shotwell
Verna Stassevitch
Pat Stemmler
Marian Wirth

CONTENTS

CONTENTS

CONTENTS

Part 1

SINGING ACTIVITIES

Children have many natural interests and talents, but one activity that appeals to all children is music and singing. Even newborn infants respond to rhythmic rocking and lullabies. Children often bounce to music before they can walk.

Add to this inborn love of music, creative body movement and language, and you have a truly marvelous mix of learning modes. In this section, a variety of styles of musical games will be presented each with its own charm and educational benefits.

Section A: Musical Fingergames

Besides the obvious benefit of giving small muscles exercise and developing fine motor control and coordination, these simple activities provide children with rich experience in humor, fantasy, problem-solving and vocal expression.

Teachers will find these fingergames particularly useful activities because most are relatively quiet and can be done while seated. They can be used to fill time when the group is waiting, and can be a calming-down activity after a more active game.

FIVE LITTLE CHICKADEES

Age: 2–5 years

Benefits: Simple math concepts:
  use of number words
  practice in counting backward, subtraction
  matching the proper number of fingers to words
  rhythm, rhyme and group fun

Directions: Children generally sit in a circle for this game; they hold up a
hand with all fingers extended. As each verse is sung, one finger
"flies away" (is folded up).

FIVE LIT-TLE CHICK-A-DEES SIT-TING ON A DOOR.

ONE FLEW A-WAY AND THEN THERE WERE FOUR.

CHICK-A-DEE, CHICK-A-DEE, HAP-PY AND GAY.

CHICK-A-DEE, CHICK-A-DEE FLY, FLY A-WAY!

Variations

1. Five children can act out the roles of the five chickadees "flying" away,
   one at a time.

2: The *chorus* could be clapped without words after each *verse*.

THE ACORN SONG

Age: 3–8 years

Benefits: Humor
Group solidarity
Coordination (tapping)

Directions: Children sit in a group or circle and sing the song together. After the word "nut," children lightly knock on their own heads twice.

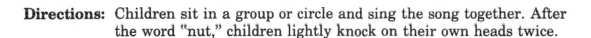

Comments: The song may be more useful at Thanksgiving or in the autumn when children are collecting and studying nuts and pods.

BILLY BOY
(Playground Song, Chant, Clapping Game)

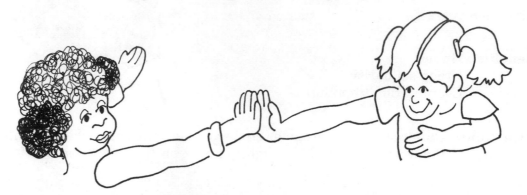

Age: 4–8 years (This song's hand motions are simpler than they appear in print.)

Benefits: Coordination of action with rhythm and words
Practice in rhyming words

Directions:

1. For pre-school children, this activity can be learned in a large group sitting in a circle on the floor.

2. Begin with a simple "clap-pat" rhythm pattern. It doesn't matter if you pat your thighs first or clap your hands. Don't use words yet.

3. After the rhythm pattern is set, begin chanting the words.

4. On the last two words, break the "clap-pat" pattern and touch your chest, then your stomach, without losing the rhythm of the chant. Young children love this surprise ending.

Code for Motions:

    o = Clap your hands
    x = Pat thighs
    TC = Touch chest
    TS = Touch own stomach

Additional Verses:

2. learned to tie his shoe   5. how to drive   8. shut the gate
3. learned to climb a tree   6. pick up sticks   9. climb a vine
4. learned to shut the door   7. walked right   10. caught a great big hen
                                   up to heaven

Variations:

1. Make up some of your own rhymes.

2. Use the song/chant as a partner activity with first, second and third graders. Follow the clap pattern suggested below or let the partners create their own.

   Code for Partner Activity:

   o = Clap own hands
   R = Partners clap right hands
   L = Partners clap left hands
   TC = Touch own chest
   TS = Touch own stomach

Comments: Primary school children can often originate complex clap patterns that the teacher will be hard put to duplicate!

DO YOUR EARS HANG LOW?

Age: 4–10 years

Benefits: Coordination—matching easy hand motions to
  rhythm and words
  Enrichment of verbal language with gesture
  language
  Humor

Directions: See Music

TUNE: TURKEY IN THE STRAW

DO YOUR EARS HANG LOW, DO THEY WOBBLE TO AND FRO? CAN YOU

TIE THEM IN A KNOT, CAN YOU TIE THEM IN A BOW? CAN YOU

THROW THEM OVER YOUR SHOUL-DER, LIKE A CONTINENTAL SOLDIER? DO YOUR

EARS HANG LOW?

Verse 2: Do your ears hang high? (Put hands by ears, fingers point up)
Do they reach up to the sky? (arms upward)
Are they curly when they're wet? (wiggle fingers around head)
Are they shaggy when they're dry? (shake hands around head)
Can you toss them over your shoulder? (tossing motion)
Like a continental soldier? (salute)
Do your ears hang high? (hands by ears, fingers upward)

Comments: The humor is so obvious that even very young children can appreciate it. This is the kind of song that children hum to themselves while working or playing. They will remember it for years. It is typically a good "in the car" song.

INKY DINKY DOO

Age: 4½–7 years

Benefits: Humor: fun names for body parts
Memory for a chain of words (built up throughout many short verses of the song)

Directions: This song adapted from an old German children's song, employs the mechanism of adding on an additional pair of words with each of many short verses resulting in a long chain of amusing body part labels. A set of pictures or a poster will help children remember the labels in the correct order.

Children touch body parts as they sing.

Verses:

2: Put my hand on my self, self.
  What do I see, see?
  This is my eye-winker,
  Oh, Mama dear.
  Eye-winker, think-boxer,
  Inky-Dinky Doo.
  That's what I learned in my school.

3: Put my hand on my self, self.
  What do I see, see?
  This is my nose-smeller,
  Oh, Mama dear.
  Nose-smeller, eye-winker, think-boxer,
  Inky Dinky Doo.
  That's what I learned in my school.

Additional Verses:

   ear-list'ner
   mouth-souper
   chest-protector
   tummy-warmer
   hip-wiggler
   knee-bender
   ankle-breaker
   foot-warmer
   kid-huggers (arms)

THINK-BOXER · EYE-WINKER · NOSE-SMELLER · MOUTH-SOUPER · EAR-LIST'NER

JACK IN THE BOX

Age: 3–5 years

Benefits: Coordination of actions and words
Opportunity for dramatic play
Development of locomotor skills—slow bending of knees followed by
a quick jump from a squatting position

Materials: None, unless you want to use a large decorated box for fun! Hiding
behind a chair can also be used as a variation.

Directions: Random positions around the room. Children lower themselves to
a squatting position, hands covering their heads. On the words,
"touch the spring" they jump or "pop up."

JACK-IN-THE-BOX IS OUT OF SIGHT, WHEN THE COVER'S FASTEN'D TIGHT;

TOUCH THE SPRING AND UP HE GOES, JACK-IN-THE-BOX WITH HIS LONG RED NOSE.

Variations:

1. Partners are scattered in random positions around the room. One partner is the "Jack in the Box" and the other is the child operating it. The
operator stands behind her partner and gently pushes him on the head
with one hand until he is in a squatting position. Then she places her
other hand on top of the head (the cover is now tight). At the words
"touch the spring," the operator releases both hands from the child's
head and the "Jack in the Box" pops up. Naturally, you have to do it
again and reverse positions!

2. Children can crouch behind a small chair to pretend they are in a box and pop up at the appropriate time.

A large cardboard box with a flip-top lid can also be decorated like a real "Jack in the Box" and one child at a time can climb in and take turns popping out.

3. Another tune to use! The descending scale pattern of the melody is excellent for the beginning actions of the game. The child, of course, pops out on "Yes, I will!"

JACK-IN-THE-BOX, STILL AS A MOUSE, DEEP DOWN IN-SIDE HIS

LIT-TLE DARK HOUSE. JACK-IN-THE-BOX, REST-ING SO STILL;

WILL YOU COME OUT? YES, I WILL!

Comments: Children, especially three-year-olds, could do this every day and never tire of it. Watch out when you use partners; the one behind must always remember to step back or be prepared to get "bumped."

ROLL OVER

Age: 3–5 years

Benefits: Use of counting and sequencing skills
Fine motor exercise: coordinating finger action with words
Vocal expression: using different voices

Directions: Have children sit in a circle so they can have a good view of each other.

Sing the song with appropriate actions, holding up the appropriate number of fingers on line 1, wiggling your little finger for the "little one," rotating both hands whenever you sing "roll over" and finally slapping your hand on your knee on the last word "out."

THERE WERE FIVE IN THE BED, AND THE LIT-TLE ONE SAID "ROLL
OV-ER, ROLL OV-ER." SO THEY ALL ROLLED OV-ER AND ONE FELL OUT —

Variations:

1. Have children think of five different "feelings": sad, angry silly, etc., and put those in place of "the little one said"; for example, "the sad one said." Then use appropriate voice for the roll-over phrase.

2. Young children love to act this out, as simple as it is. Have five children lie on the floor in the middle of a circle, rolling, one on each verse, right out of the circle.
   To make a bigger production of this, combine Variation 2 with the idea in Variation 1, and give each child a speaking part: saying, "roll over" in an assumed voice.

3. After doing this fingerplay for awhile, provide a *new* ending and have the group sing: "I've got the whole bed to myself," sung to the tune of: "He's got the whole world in his hands."

4. Reverse the procedure and add people to the bed, beginning with "*one* in the bed and the little one said: I'm lonely. So he/she scooted right over and another got in."

5. Have your children "act out" the fingerplay using Variation 4. Each child in the group will get a chance to jump into the bed and will get the speaking part, "I'm lonely." To make it even more fun, you can make a small space on the floor and designate that as the bed. Will everybody fit? All might have to "scrunch" together, but that's a good lesson in cooperation.

THERE WERE FIVE IN THE BED . . .

Comments: Young children enjoy familiar activities, and the repetition of those they enjoy is important. This fingerplay becomes familiar quickly, and can then be changed and modified so it's still entertaining for everybody for a long period of time.

TINY TIM

Age: 4–10 years

Benefits: Humor, group solidarity and fun
Opportunity for dramatic play

Directions: Choose a child to act the easy part of Tiny Tim; choose others for the doctor, the nurse, and the lady with the alligator purse. The remainder of the children can sing and act out some motions of the verses.

Materials: None. The doctor, nurse and lady could carry bags if you wish.

Comments: This song (or it may be a chant) is very popular as a jump-rope rhyme that children have giggled over for many years, perhaps for a generation or two. Why is it so popular? Because the rhythm is easy and strong, but mostly because it makes light of sibling rivalry and illness. It somehow reassures children that it's okay to have less than affectionate feelings toward their own siblings.

Make sure that all children eventually get a turn playing one of the major parts, not necessarily on the same day.

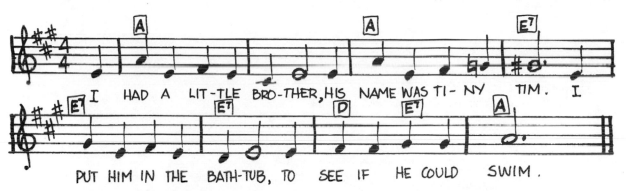

BALL-BOUNCING SONG

I HAD A LIT-TLE BRO-THER, HIS NAME WAS TI-NY TIM. I
PUT HIM IN THE BATH-TUB, TO SEE IF HE COULD SWIM.

2. He drank up all the water,
   He ate up all the soap,
   He died the next morning,
   (or his tummy hurt that evening)
   With a bubble in his throat.

3. In came the doctor,
   In came the nurse,
   In came the lady
   with the alligator purse.

4. "Measles," said the doctor,
   "Mumps," said the nurse,
   "Chickenpox," said the lady
   with the alligator purse.

5. "Penicillin," said the doctor,
   "penicillin," said the nurse,
   "penicillin," said the lady
   with the alligator purse.

6. "I don't want the doctor!
   I don't want the nurse!
   I don't want the lady
   with the alligator purse!"

7. Out walked the doctor,
   Out walked the nurse,
   Out walked the lady,
   with the alligator purse.

Section B: Active Musical Games

Perhaps these games, in which children are up and moving around, are the most beneficial because whole body control is added to the other benefits.

Teachers will find comfort in the fact that many of these songs are familiar old tunes with a new twist. Sometimes teachers seem reluctant to introduce a very active game for fear of losing control of the class. The best preventative measures are:

1. The teacher should have the game's directions in mind well ahead of time.

2. The teacher should not expect a perfect performance. Allow the game to be somewhat sloppy while the children are learning it.

Children who know a wide variety of active games are indeed fortunate. What a wonderful way to develop confidence, body control, ability to listen and follow directions, and social give and take.

CHATTER WITH THE ANGELS

Age: 5–8 years

Benefits: Coordination of action and words
Development of quick reactions (thinking ahead)
Awareness of body parts
Development of locomotor skills

CHAT-TER WITH THE AN-GELS SOON IN THE MORN-ING, CHAT-TER WITH THE AN-GELS IN THAT LAND.

CHAT-TER WITH THE AN-GELS SOON IN THE MORN-ING, CHAT-TER WITH THE AN-GELS, JOIN THE BAND.

I HOPE TO JOIN THAT BAND AND CHAT-TER WITH THE AN-GELS ALL DAY LONG!

I HOPE TO JOIN THAT BAND AND CHAT-TER WITH THE AN-GELS ALL DAY LONG!

Additional Verses:

2. March with the angels, etc.   4. Dance with the angels, etc.
3. Skip with the angels, etc.   5. Tiptoe with the angels, etc.

6. Clap with the angels, etc.   8. Tap with the angels, etc.
7. Click with the angels, etc.   9. Whistle with the angels, etc.

How many more verses can the children think of?

Directions: Sing the song through and have the children notice the two spots in the song where they sing, "I hope to join that band." Tell them they must always stop what they are doing while they *sing* those words, and then continue the action or movement until those words appear again. It is like a game of "stop and go" and keeps everyone on his/her toes. Try sitting-down actions first until everyone gets the idea, then try marching, skipping, etc.

Variation: Make a game out of this activity. Anyone moving or making a body sound on the two *singing* phrases, "I hope to join that band," is automatically out of the game.

Comments: No one can sit still when you start singing this song! It's lots of fun, but it takes some thinking.

THE COBBLER SONG

Age: 3–6 years

Benefits: Development of coordination skills
Development of locomotor skills
Development of "rhythmic feel"
Coordination of actions with music
Opportunity for imaginative play

Directions: Children sit in a circle and teacher starts to tell the story:

In the early days, the shoemaker was called a "cobbler." He didn't have all the fancy tools and machines that we have today; he had to do everything by hand. To help make the work go a little faster, he would sing while he was working on the shoes.

(Pound one fist on top of the other while telling the story and continue to "pound" during the first verse of the song. (Children will join in with actions.)

TRADITIONAL

COB-BLER, COB-BLER, MEND MY SHOE . GET IT DONE BY HALF PAST TWO . TOUR-A LOUR-A LOUR-A LU .

STITCH IT UP AND STITCH IT DOWN, WHILE I'M GOING ROUND THE TOWN . TOUR-A LOUR-A LOUR-A LU .

Sing song 3 times, changing movements each time.

1st line: Pound fists on top of each other.
2nd line: Move arm and hand up and down as if you are sewing.
1st line: Pound floor and thighs.
2nd line: Clap and snap fingers going up and down.
1st line: Stand up and bend on knees.
2nd line: Go up and down on toes.

Variation: After singing the song, take a trip to an imaginary shoe store and try on shoes: some that are too big, too small, that make you walk on your toes or heels, etc. The children can also suggest different types of shoes.

DILLY—DILLY

Age: 4½–7 years

Benefits: Following a simple sequence of motions and coordinating them with words and music

Developing social skills: coordinating the song's motions with a partner

Materials: None; however, marking two rear boundary lines on the floor with rope, chalk or masking tape is helpful while learning the game.

THIS IS HOW WE DILLY, DILLY (MOVING ARMS UP AND DOWN IN A CHOPPING MOTION)

Directions: Start with a small group first (4 to 6 children). Add more gradually.

Practice motions without music and music without motions before putting it all together.

Children stand in 2 lines, about 4 feet apart, facing their partners. Allow space to each side of each child.

Verses:	*Motions*
1. This is how we dilly, dilly; etc.	Children hold arms straight out in front and "chop" arms up and down while singing the first verse.
2. Jump back, Sally, Sally; etc.	Children jump backwards a few inches on each beat, until the rows are about 8–10 feet apart. (Children may end up standing on a boundary line if desired.)
3. Walkin' thru the alley, alley; etc.	Children do-si-do (arms folded on chest, partners approach each other in the center space, pass around each other, and each backs up to his or her original place near the boundary line).
4. Here comes Bill and Jerry; etc.	The two children at the foot of the lines (rows) skip up to the top of the lines and take new places there. The other children move down a little and the song resumes until all children have had a turn skipping through the "alley."

Comments: This is similar to a very simple form of square dance, but don't tell the children this or it will sound too hard.

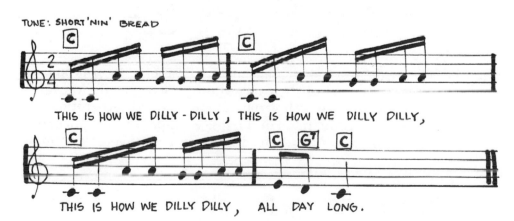

HELLO! HOW ARE YOU? (I)

Age: 2–6 years

Benefits: Each child receives recognition
Group solidarity and individual self-esteem are developed
Greetings and affection are given and received

Directions: Children sit in a circle. The song is started and, as each child's name is sung, he or she might raise a hand and wave, or nod the head or perform whatever motion you want the child to practice, to indicate recognition.

(TO THE TUNE OF: "SKIP TO MY LOU ")

HEL-LO HOW ARE YOU? HEL-LO HOW ARE YOU? HEL-LO HOW ARE YOU?

HOW ARE YOU TO- DAY? IT'S GOOD TO SEE NIC-KY BACK, IT'S GOOD TO SEE IV-AN BACK, IT'S

GOOD TO SEE LA- KI-SHA BACK, CONTINUE AROUND CIRCLE HOW ARE YOU TO- DAY?

HELLO! HOW ARE YOU TODAY?

Comments: Have you ever, as an adult, entered a room full of people and had no one say "Hello"? It is important for every child in every school or center to have both verbal and non-verbal recognition as he/she arrives each day. In addition, this song provides a quick, easy way for teachers *and* children collectively to notice each child and say his/her name.

HELLO, HOW ARE YOU? (II)

Age: 3–6 years

Benefits: Social interaction
Development of motor skills

Directions: Move freely around the room while singing and shaking hands (everyone moves and everyone shakes hands). At the end of the first verse, whomever you are shaking hands with becomes your partner and you do the movement directions together. Change the movement direction each time you sing the song so you will have a new partner and a new movement each time.

Song: Tune of "Skip To My Lou"

Hello, how are you?
Hello, how are you?
Hello, how are you?
How are you my darlin'?
(*At this point, take a partner.*)

Walk, walk, walk, to my Lou
Walk, walk, walk, to my Lou
Walk, walk, walk, to my Lou
Walk to my Lou, my darlin'.

Variation: Very young children can all sit on the floor in a circle as the teacher goes around and shakes everyone's hand. As the teacher passes students, they turn and shake hands with children on either side of them. Instead of movement, use body percussion such as clapping, patting thighs, touching the floor or moving arms.

Comments: This is a good get-acquainted activity.

I'M A LITTLE DUTCH CHILD

Age: 4–8 years

Benefits: Strenuous leg exercise (rhythmic kicks)
Matching actions with words
Practice in acting out a simple part:
     coming in on cue
     following a simple story sequence

Directions: Half the group stands in a long line, facing the other half of the group. The rows are about 4 feet apart to provide kicking room.

Group 1 sings the first verse and kicks rhythmically while standing in place. Group 2 listens.

I'M A LITTLE DUTCH CHILD, DUTCH CHILD, DUTCH CHILD. I'M A LITTLE DUTCH CHILD, HI HO SEE!

Now Group 2 sings the second verse, and kicks rhythmically while group 1 listens. The two groups alternate verses until the last verse, when all sing and kick together.

Group 2: I'm a little Dutch child, Dutch child, Dutch child
I'm a little Dutch child, hi, ho, see!

Group 1: We do not like you, like you, like you.
We do not like you, hi, ho, see!

Group 2: Why don't you like us, like us, like us? etc.

Group 1: Because you stole our cookies, cookies, cookies, etc.

Group 2: Will you please forgive us, forgive us, forgive us?

Group 1: Yes, we will forgive you, forgive you, forgive you, etc.

Both Groups: Now we're all together, together, together, etc.

Comments: This is a good way for children to get lots of physical release indoors. Therefore, it's a good rainy day activity.

JENNY CRACK CORN

Age: 3–6 years

Benefits: Awareness of body parts
Awareness of left, right and other directions
Practice in following a series of directions
Coordination of words and actions

AMERICAN SINGING GAME

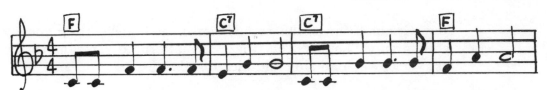

JEN-NY CRACK CORN AND I DON'T CARE. JEN-NY CRACK CORN AND I DON'T CARE.

JEN-NY CRACK CORN AND I DON'T CARE, TO-DAY'S A HOL-I-DAY.

Verses:

1. Round and round and I don't care,
   Round and round and I don't care,
   Round and round and I don't care,
   Now let's all stand still.

2. Right hand up and I don't care,
   Right hand up and I don't care,
   Right hand up and I don't care,
   Turn the other way.

3. Left hand up and I don't care,
   Left hand up and I don't care,
   Left hand up and I don't care,
   Turn right back again.

4. Both hands up and I don't care,
   Both hands up and I don't care,
   Both hands up and I don't care,
   Circle round again (sing chorus again).

Directions: Single circle formation. All children sing and clap hands as they sing the chorus. During the first verse, they skip around in the circle. Then they stand and make the appropriate motions for the remaining verses.

Variations: You may like to play this game on the spur of the moment. Children can be at random places in the room and the directions for each verse can be done individually (Example: "round and round" would be turning around in place). Add many more verses such as:

Wiggle your nose and I don't care
Pat your head and I don't care
Touch your spine and I don't care
Bend your wrist and I don't care
Nod your head and I don't care
Bend your knees and I don't care

Comments: You might want to learn the song about the "Blue-Tail Fly," which has the "Jimmy Crack Corn" chorus as a part of it.

JIM ALONG JOSIE

Age: 3½–10 years

Benefits: Rhythmic coordination of body
Practice of various locomotor movements, one for each verse of the song
Language development through story-telling and song

Materials: Instruments may be used, but are not necessary.

Directions: Children may start in a circle, walking for the first verse. Then they may hop, run, skip, etc., in a circle formation or move freely around the room. Change the tempo (speed) of the song with each new locomotor activity.

Verses:

1. Hop, hop along, Jim along Josie
   Hop, hop along, Jim along Joe.

2. Run, run along, Jim along Josie
   Run, run along, Jim along Joe.

3. Crawl, crawl along, Jim along Josie
   Crawl, crawl along, Jim along Joe.

4. Walk, walk along, Jim along Josie
   Walk, walk along, Jim along Joe.

   Jump—Roll—Skip—Tip Toe, etc.

Variation: Choose a different rhythm instrument to accompany each verse.

Comments: You can adapt the song in order to tell a simple story, such as:

> We're going swimming, swimming, Josie;
> We're going swimming later today.
> We'll have a picnic, picnic, Josie;
> We'll play baseball, Jim along Joe.

Or you may use the song for smoothing a transition:

> Time to clean up now, Jim along Josie;
> Time to clean up now, Jim along Joe.
> Put all the games away, Jim along Josie;
> It's time for snack, now, Jim along Joe.

A LETTER, A LETTER

Age: 3–5 years

Benefits: Letter recognition
Body awareness in different types of space
Coordination
Gross motor skills such as running

Directions: Sing the song through and at the end each child is to make the letter called for by the teacher or leader. He or she is to use any or all parts of his body in any position (lying down, sitting or standing, etc.) to form the letter.

Encourage many creative uses of limbs. This can be done by asking for the same letter twice, and requesting a different version the second time. For children just beginning letter recognition, you could hold up a copy of the letter on a card as you call out the name at the end of each verse. Children can be the leaders in this activity also.

(TUNE A TISKET, A TASKET)

A LET-TER, A. LET-TER, I CAN MAKE A LET-TER. I

TAKE MY ARMS AND TAKE MY LEGS AND I CAN MAKE A ___
(P,B,T,O,ETC)

Variation: "A-Tisket, A-Tasket" is the well-known version of this folk song. The game accompanying it is also an old, but very popular, activity. The song and directions follow.

Directions: This is a "drop the handkerchief" game. Form a single circle, with children holding hands. The child who is "it" carries a handkerchief (or scarf or letter) as he runs around the outside of the circle and the rest sing. He drops the handkerchief behind the person of his choice, then continues running around the circle. The other child immediately runs in the opposite direction around the outside of the circle. Each tries to reach the vacant place first. The one who fails picks up the handkerchief and is "it" for the next play of the game. (You will notice some children find it hard to remember to go in the "opposite" direction when they are chosen. This activity is good reinforcement for this concept.)

A TIS-KET, A TAS-KET, A GREEN AND YEL-LOW BAS-KET, I WROTE A LET-TER TO MY LOVE AND ON THE WAY I DROPPED IT; I DROPPED IT, I DROPPED IT, AND ON THE WAY I DROPPED IT; A LIT-TLE PERSON PICKED IT UP AND PUT IT IN HIS POC-KET.

Comments: A sample of how you can use a very simple, familiar tune in two completely different activities.

LITTLE RED CABOOSE

Age: 2–6 years

For: Rhythmic coordination of body
Body awareness in a moving group:
        (giving self and others adequate space)
Unity of language and motions
Group togetherness
(This song can help with transitions from one place to another.)

Directions: Children line up, four, five or six to a train. They lightly grasp the shoulders of the child in front, and away they go, rhythmically shuffling their feet, singing and watching other trains with delight.

CAMP SONG

LIT-TLE RED CA-BOOSE, CHOO-CHOO-CHOO, LIT-TLE RED CA-BOOSE, CHOO CHOO CHOO, LITTLE RED CA-BOOSE BE-HIND THE

TRA-A-A-AIN. SMOKE STACK ON ITS BACK, CHOO-CHOO-CHOO; COM-ING DOWN THE TRACK, CHOO-CHOO-CHOO;

LIT-TLE RED CA-BOOSE BE-HIND THE   TRAIN.

Variation: Children of kindergarten age may lightly grasp the *elbows* of the child in front, and all children can rotate arms "choo-choo" style, while also shuffling feet. It is *not* necessary to insist on perfect matching of foot movements to rhythm. Most preschoolers can't do it.

POP GOES THE WEASEL

Age: 3–8 years

Benefits: Auditory skills
Quick reactions, thinking ahead
Practice in following a simple sequence of directions
Motor skills

Directions: Sing the song several times, each time doing something different on the word "pop": clap, smack your lips, make a "pop" sound with your finger in your mouth (cheek), use complete silence, jump, hop, etc. Children can suggest what other actions or movements could be done with the song.

AMERICAN SQUARE DANCE SONG

ALL A-ROUND THE COB-BLER'S BENCH, THE MON-KEY CHASED THE WEA-SEL. THE
MON-KEY THOUGHT 'TWAS ALL IN FUN. POP! GOES THE WEA-SEL.

Song: All around the Cobbler's bench,
The monkey chased the weasel.
The monkey thought 'twas all in fun
Pop goes the weasel.

A penny for a spool of thread,
A penny for a needle.
That's the way the money goes
Pop goes the weasel.

Variation:

1. Use simple rhythm instruments or homemade instruments and play only on "Pop." Repeat, but play on everything *except* "Pop."

2. For added fun and suspense, children must wait a second or two for a special signal from the teacher before doing their "Pop" motion. For example, everyone agrees to jump up high on the word "pop." Sing the song as usual, but all pause after the word, "fun." Everyone waits in delightful anticipation, then the teacher gives the "go-ahead" signal (points a finger) and everyone pops up high. The longer the pause, the more fun it is.

MISS POLLY HAD A DOLLY

Age: 3–6 years

For: Accompanying words and music with another form of communication—
the gesture
Telling a simply-organized story in sequence
Remembering what comes next and getting ready

Materials: None necessary but, if desired, the doctor could have a bag, hat and
a paper bill.

Directions: The easy version calls for each child to act out all the parts while
seated (Miss Polly, the dolly, the doctor). A slightly more complicated version calls for one child to be the dolly, another child to
act out Miss Polly and a third child can be the doctor. All the children sing for this second version. Remember to have girl doctors
part of the time and boy dollies.

THE "DOLLY", "MISS POLLY" AND THE "DOCTOR"

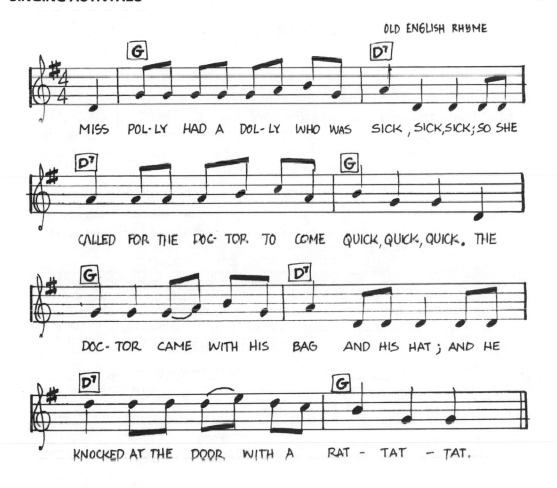

Verse 2:

He looked at the dolly and he shook his head; (shake head)
Then he said, "Miss Polly, put her straight to bed." (shake finger)
He wrote on a paper for a pill, pill, pill; (writing motions)
"I'll be back in the morning with my bill, bill, bill." (hand Polly the bill)

Variation: Sing the song as in Version 1, but stay silent on the last three words of each line, and clap 3 times instead.

MY DOLLY

Age: 3–5 years

Benefits: Opportunity for imaginative play
Development of locomotor skills—different styles of walking, marching, dancing, etc.
Control of simple musical instruments

Materials: None except for variation (rhythm instruments such as sticks, drums, triangles, wood blocks, cymbals and tambourines)

1. I HAVE A LIT-TLE DOL-LY AND SHE WALKS, AND SHE WALKS, AND SHE WALKS. SHE'S A
2. I HAVE A LIT-TLE DOL-LY AND SHE TALKS:"MA-MA", AND SHE TALKS:"MA-MA", AND SHE TALKS:"MA-MA", SHE'S A

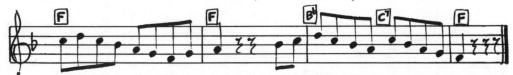

CUN-NING LIT-TLE DOL-LY WHEN SHE WALKS. SHE'S A CUN-NING LIT-TLE DOL-LY WHEN SHE WALKS.
CUN-NING LIT-TLE DOL-LY WHEN SHE TALKS:"MA-MA". SHE'S A CUN-NING LIT-TLE DOL-LY WHEN SHE TALKS:"MA-MA".

"AND SHE WALKS..."

"AND SHE TALKS..."

"AND SHE DANCES..."

Directions: In Verse 1, the legs should be stiff when walking and the arms bent at the elbows, moving up and down like sticks.

Verse 2: keep the same body position as in Verse 1. On, "Ma Ma," bend upper part of body forward stiffly as you say the words.

Additional Verses:

3. I have a little dolly and she cries "Boo hoo" (children rub their eyes with very stiff arm motions).
4. I have a little dolly and she dances (they do a pirouette).
5. I have a GI Joe and he can march "left, right" (they march with stiff legs).
6. I have a GI Joe and he salutes "Yes, Sir!" (the children salute with a very stiff arm).

Variation: The use of rhythm instruments to accompany the verses adds to the imaginative toylike movements.

Verses:

1. rhythm sticks or woodblocks tapping the beat.
2. tambourines (shake them only on "Ma Ma").
3. finger cymbals on "Boo hoo."
4. triangles all the way through this verse.
5. drums keeping the beat.
6. drum plays only on the "Yes, Sir!"

This song could be expanded to include all kinds of toys, especially animals.

Comments: It's as old as the hills, but children love it!

THE OLD GREY CATS ARE SLEEPING

Age: 3–6 years

Benefits: Concentration and listening for signals;
Practice in acting out a simple story which changes from very quiet
to boisterous;
Motor skills; such as running and chasing

(THE OLD GREY CATS ARE SLEEPING; THE LITTLE MICE COME CREEPING.)

Directions:

1. Half the children can pretend to be the cats; half will be mice. During
the first verse (see music), the cats yawn, stretch and curl up to sleep on
the rug. The mice wait at one side of the room for the cats to get to
sleep.

2. The mice sing: "The little mice are creeping, creeping, creeping," etc. As they sing, the mice come out and tip-toe around the room.

3. The mice pretend to eat, singing: "The little mice are nibbling, nibbling, nibbling," etc.

4. The cats begin to stir, yawn, stretch, wake up, and watch the mice. The cats (or everyone) sing: "The old grey cats are waking, waking, waking," etc.

5. Now, everyone runs lightly, the cats chasing the mice back "home," singing very fast: "The little mice are running, running, running," etc.

End: Since the cats usually don't catch the mice, the teacher can put out bowls of cream for all the cats.

Comments: Everyone gets a good part in this act-out song. And you can be sure everyone will squeal and giggle when the cats wake up and chase the mice. In this activity, preschoolers will practice the important skill of expressing themselves through action and gesture, an important part of language and communications.

TRADITIONAL AMERICAN

THE OLD GREY CATS ARE SLEEP-ING, SLEEP-ING, SLEEP-ING. THE

OLD GREY CATS ARE SLEEP-ING, IN THE HOUSE.

OLD JOE CLARK

Age: 3 years through elementary grades

Benefits: Development of humor through nonsense rhymes
Development of locomotor skills

Directions: Children walk, run lightly, skip, jump or hop during the refrain.
They stand still during the stanza.

REFRAIN (children move as they sing)   American fiddle tune

ROUND A-ROUND OLD JOE CLARK,   ROUND A-ROUND I SAY.

ROUND A-ROUND OLD JOE CLARK, I AIN'T GOT LONG TO STAY.

STANZA (children stand still and clap as they sing the stanza)

OLD JOE CLARK HE HAD A HOUSE,   SIX-TEEN STO-RIES HIGH.

EV-RY STO-RY IN THAT HOUSE WAS FULL OF CHIC-KEN PIE.

Old Joe Clark he had a dog,
As blind as he could be,
Chased a redbug 'round a stump,
And a coon up a hollow tree.

I went down to Old Joe's house,
Never been there before,
He slept on the feather bed,
And I slept on the floor.

Old Joe Clark he had a cat,
Smart as he could be,
Taught him how to add and subtract,
And to multiply by three.

Old Joe Clark he had a wife,
As blind as she could be,
She chased him round the backyard pump,
And then up a hickory tree.

Variations:

1. Have your children help you make up your own stanzas about Old Joe Clark.
2. Ruth C. Seeger[1] suggests the following variation: For the refrain, suggest actions such as clapping, tapping, stamping, nodding, shaking, etc. Continue the action through both refrain and stanza, singing la-la-la instead of words in the stanza. For example:

   Refrain: Clap, clap, clap your hands
   Clap your hands together;
   Clap, clap, clap your hands;
   Clap your hands together.

   Stanza: Children continue clapping and singing la-la-la.

Comments: This tune seems to be known by everyone and any activity you try with it will have instant success. This is a good stop-and-go activity.

---

[1]Ruth C. Seeger, *American Folk Songs for Children*, Garden City, N.Y., Doubleday & Co., Inc., 1948.

OLD MAC DONALD HAD A BAND

Age: 3–8 years

Benefits: Awareness of body parts
Awareness of body sounds

TUNE: OLD MAC DONALD HAD A FARM

OLD MAC DONALD HAD A BAND, E - I - E - I - OH.   AND

IN THIS BAND HE   HAD SOME FEET, E - I - E - I - OH . WITH A

STAMP, STAMP HERE ; STAMP, STAMP THERE ; HERE A STAMP, THERE A STAMP,

EV-RY WHERE A STAMP, STAMP . OLD MAC DONALD HAD A BAND, E - I - E - I - OH .

Directions: Can be done standing or sitting in a circle. Mention to the children that you are going to sing a song about Old Mac Donald, but instead of a farm, he had a band! This band consisted of body parts. Start with hands or feet in the band. The children will immediately join in the actions and sounds because they are very easy to follow. Some suggestions for body parts and sounds:

> mouth—smack, smack
> nose—sniff, sniff
> eyes—blink, blink
> ears—pull, pull (pull on ears)

Ask the children for suggestions to continue with body parts and sounds. I ended the song with:

> And in this band he had a *body,* E-I-EI-O
> With a wiggle, wiggle here and a wiggle, wiggle there
> (move the whole body), etc.

Comments: This is such a fun activity, we even did it with the parents on "Open House" night and they also enjoyed it.

ROW YOUR BOAT

Age: 3–8 years

Benefits: Combination of song and movement
Awareness of crossover, forward, backward and sideward

Materials: Simple rhythm instruments: tone blocks, rhythm sticks, castanets, maracas, bells, finger cymbals and triangles.

ROW-ROW-ROW YOUR BOAT, GENT-LY DOWN THE STREAM.

MER-RI-LY, MER-RI-LY, MER-RI-LY, MER-RI-LY; LIFE IS BUT A DREAM.

Directions: Children sit in a circle on the floor. Sing the song 4 times: 3 times with different actions or movements and the last time with instruments.

1. Sing song and "row" 4 times on each side of body for each phrase. (16 "rows" in all)

ROW, ROW, ROW YOUR BOAT.

2. Sing song with following actions for each phrase:
   a. "Swim" forward with arms.
   b. "Swim" backward with arms.
   c. Swing arms side to side (make sure you cross the midline each time).
   d. Put both hands together, lean to one side and rest head on hands, as if going to sleep.

3. Take a partner and sit on the floor facing partner. Hold partners' hands and "pull" each other back and forth while singing the song.

4. Use rhythm instruments for each phrase:
   a. rhythm sticks, tone blocks, castanets
   b. maracas and any other "shakers"
   c. bells
   d. finger cymbals and triangles

"SCOOTING" ROW

Variation: Eliminate words and just have the instruments play for each phrase. The teacher should establish a beat and give a signal to start. Each group of instruments will "sound" 4 times (once for each beat).

Comments: Even older children love this song. They can sing and "row" their boat to someplace special (Example: a jungle or foreign country) and then discuss sounds or activities common to that place, then "row" back home.

A SAILOR WENT TO SEA, SEA, SEA

Age: 2½–7 years

Benefits: Simultaneous match of rhythm, words, actions and visual monitoring
Body awareness: tapping various body parts
Simple humor in words and actions
Social skills: finding pleasure in following an organized sequence
(plan of action) in a group
Quick reactions (especially last verse)

A SAILOR WENT TO SEA-SEA-SEA, TO SEE WHAT HE COULD SEE-SEE-SEE, AND

ALL THAT HE COULD SEE-SEE-SEE, WAS THE DEEP DARK BOT-TOM OF THE SEA-SEA-SEA.

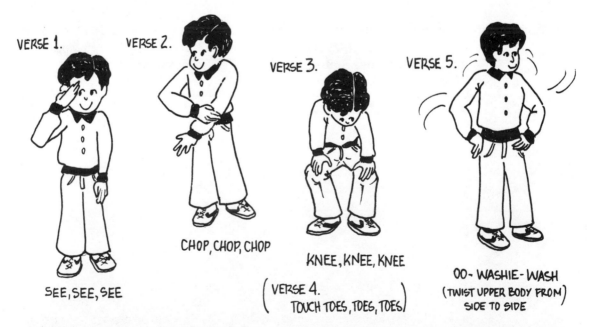

VERSE 1. SEE, SEE, SEE

VERSE 2. CHOP, CHOP, CHOP

VERSE 3. KNEE, KNEE, KNEE

(VERSE 4. TOUCH TOES, TOES, TOES)

VERSE 5. OO-WASHIE-WASH (TWIST UPPER BODY FROM SIDE TO SIDE)

Directions: First practice in slow motion all body movements (see below) before doing the song. The teacher can set a slow pace at first.

Verses:

Actions:

1. A sailor went to sea, sea, sea;
   To see what he could see, see, see.
   And all that he could see, see, see;
   Was the deep, dark bottom of the sea, sea, sea.

   With hand in "salute" position, children tap their foreheads three times on each "see, see, see."

2. A sailor went to chop, chop, chop,
   To see what he could chop, chop, chop.
   And all that he could chop, chop, chop,
   Was the deep, dark bottom of the chop, chop, chop.

   Tap left arm with right hand three times on each "chop, chop, chop."

3. A sailor went to knee, knee, knee,
   To see what he could knee, knee, knee.
   And all that he could knee, knee, knee,
   Was the deep, dark bottom of the knee, knee,
       knee.

   Pat knees three times, with open hand on each "knee, knee, knee."

4. A sailor went to toe, toe, toe,
   To see what he could toe, toe, toe.
   And all that he could toe, toe, toe,
   Was the deep, dark bottom of the toe, toe, toe.

   Children touch toes three times on each "toe, toe, toe."

5. A sailor went to oo-washie-wash,
   To see what he could oo-washie-wash.
   But all that he could oo-washie-wash,
   Was the deep, dark bottom of the oo-washie-wash.

   Children place hands on hips and, with feet planted firmly on the floor, twist bodies to the left, to the right and again to the left, on the "oo-washie-wash."

(omit for two-year-olds)

6. A sailor went to see, chop, knee, toe,
   oo-washie-wash:
   To see what he could see, chop, knee, toe,
   oo-washie-wash,
   And all that he could see, chop, knee, toe,
   oo-washie-wash,
   Was the deep, dark bottom of the sea, chop,
   knee, toe, oo-washie-wash.

   Children touch in quick succession: forehead, arm, knee, toe, then swing hips on "oo-washie-wash."

Comments: This song has just enough action to make it challenging for older children, yet it can be slowed down to make it easy for very young ones. All children are enchanted with the "oo-washie-wash" movement, an imitation of the washing machine's agitator. Children also love the challenge of the funny last verse.

THE SHOEMAKER

Age: 5–8 years

Benefits: Practice in following directions
Combination of axial and locomotor movements
Coordination of actions and words
Opportunity to work with a partner
Social awareness and language development through use of the motions and words of a shoemaker's trade

Directions: Double circle of partners facing one another, with one partner's back to the center of the circle.

"WIND IT..."

"PULL, PULL" ... "TAP, TAP, TAP" ...

" TRA LA LA LA "

Measures:

1. Revolve closed fists forward around one another.
2. Revolve closed fists backward around one another.
3. Jerk elbows back twice, vigorously.
4. Strike one clenched fist with the other three times.

> (All these actions represent the winding and pulling of the waxed thread and the driving of the pegs.)

5–8. Repeat the above actions.

9–12. Partners join both hands and take 8 skipping steps in one direction.

13–16. Partners continue to hold both hands, reverse and take 8 skipping steps in the other direction.

Variations:

1: It is sometimes fun to repeat the first part of the song again (Measures 1–8) and end with a bow to your partner.

2: With older children, you can try another skipping pattern during Measures 9–16. Partners would join inside hands and skip around the circle in a counter-clockwise direction (Measures 9–12).

On Measures 13–16, they turn in place, join other inside hands and skip back to place in a clockwise direction.

Comments: This is a very old folk dance that is easy enough for 5-year-olds to do enthusiastically and well. It's a "helper" song about a figure few children recognize today.

THE SNAIL

Age: 5–8 years

Benefits: Pratice in following directions
Development of spatial awareness
Group concentration

VERSE 1. (WIND-UP)   VERSE 2. (UNWIND)

Directions: Form a single circle, facing in one direction. All except two players join hands: one of these must be the leader. During the first verse, the leader, followed by all the others with joined hands, keeps walking in a smaller and smaller circle, in spiral form, until the entire line is wound up like the spring of a clock, with the leader at the very center. During the second verse the leader turns and, still holding the hands of the others, counter-marches his/her way through the winding opening of the spiral or "snail shell," until the players are again in one long line or circle.

HA-ND IN HAND, YOU SEE US WELL, CREEP LIKE A SNAIL IN-TO HIS SHELL.

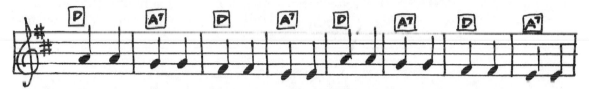

EV-ER NEAR-ER, EV-ER NEAR-ER, EV-ER CLO-SER, EV-ER CLO-SER,

VE-RY SNUG IN-DEED YOU DWELL, SNAIL WITH-IN YOUR TI-NY SHELL.

Variations:

1: The leader may draw the line out from the center by going directly through the line under the raised arms of the players, who form the rings about him as though the snail were passing through a hole in the side of his shell.

2: Running or skipping this pattern is an activity children enjoy. Play the music faster or use another, faster tune.

Comments: This is a wonderful way to define a "spiral," and a first-hand look at a small animal's home.

TEN LITTLE INDIANS

Age: 3–6 years

Benefits: Finger dexterity and small-muscle development
Opportunity for imaginative play

Directions: Children sit in circle with the teacher. Practice holding up appropriate fingers to the numbers. Practice actions to correspond with other verses, then stand in a circle.

ONE LIT-TLE, TWO LIT-TLE, THREE LIT-TLE INDIANS; FOUR LIT-TLE FIVE LIT-TLE SIX LITTLE INDIANS.

SEVEN LIT-TLE, EIGHT LIT-TLE, NINE LIT-TLE INDIANS, TEN LIT-TLE INDIAN BOYS AND GIRLS.

Song: One little, two little, three little Indians
Four little, five little, six little Indians
Seven little, eight little, nine little Indians
Ten little Indian boys and girls.

In the spring, they hoe their gardens   (Pretend to use a hoe.)
In the spring, they hoe their gardens
In the spring, they hoe their gardens
Ten little Indian boys and girls.

In the summer, they go on the warpath   (Hop up and down and
In the summer, they go on the warpath   put your hand to your
In the summer, they go on the warpath   mouth.)
Ten little Indian boys and girls.

In the fall, they build their wigwams   (Pretend to pick up poles
In the fall, they build their wigwams   and plant them in the
In the fall, they build their wigwams   ground.)
Ten little Indian boys and girls.

In the winter they build their fires   (Bend down and make a
In the winter they build their fires   sweeping motion with your
In the winter they build their fires   hands for "gathering up" fire
Ten little Indian boys and girls.   wood in one spot.)

Sit down and go back to finger play:

Ten little Indians climbing up a vine, one fell down and then there were 9.

Nine little Indians swinging on a gate, one fell off and then there were 8.

Eight little Indians climbing up to heaven, one fell down and then there were 7.

Seven little Indians playing with sticks, one got hurt and then there were 6.

Six little Indians playing 'round a hive, one got stung and then there were 5.

Five little Indians playing with a door, one fell off and then there were 4.

Four little Indians climbing up a tree, one fell down and then there were 3.

Three little Indians playing with a shoe, one fell in and then there were 2.

Two little Indians on the run, one fell down and then there was 1.

One little Indian boy or girl.

Variation: Other verses could be added: sewing beadwork, grinding corn, drying meat strips, etc.

Comments: The song ends with "boys and girls" at the request of one of the little girls in class who was tired of hearing "boys" all the time!

THE THREAD FOLLOWS THE NEEDLE

Age: 5–8 years with a variation for younger children (See Variations.)

Benefits: Practice in following directions
Coordination of actions and words
Group concentration
Gross motor experience of a fine-motor skill

THE THREAD FOL-LOWS THE NEE-DLE. THE THREAD FOL-LOWS THE NEE-DLE.

IN AND OUT THE NEE-DLE GOES, AS MO-O-THER ME-NDS THE CHIL-DREN'S CLOTHES.

Directions: Single lines of about ten children each. Hands are joined and never dropped.

Number 10 stands in place, Number 1 is the leader. With a light walking step, Number 1 walks down the front of the line and passes under the raised arms of Numbers 9 and 10, drawing the children, Numbers 2 to 8, after him/her. After they have passed under the arch, Numbers 9 and 10, keeping the hands joined, face in the opposite direction and stand with their arms crossed on their chests. This starts a kind of "chain stitch." The leader walks to his former position, and then passing in front as before, walks between Numbers 8 and 9. Number 8 then turns and adds a "stitch" to the chain. This continues and the song is repeated until all the children in line have turned about in this manner. The leader, having passed under every arch in the line, then turns under his/her own arm. Result: all the children have faced about and all their arms are crossed on their chests, making a chain.

At a signal, the children all turn about and drop their hands quickly, thus unraveling the chain and ripping out the stitches.

Variations:

1: The older children can work with longer lines and can very often play this game with a running step.

2: Children aged 2, 3 and 4 can simply join hands and the line can wind around the room, in and out a row of widely-spaced chairs, perhaps *under* a table or broom handle, or other obstacles, without dropping hands.

Comments: This is a very old singing game dating back to the turn-of-the-century.

WHAT SHALL WE DO WHEN WE ALL GO OUT?

Age: 3–5 years

Benefits: Development of locomotor skills such as hopping, jumping, crawling, climbing, running, skipping, digging, sliding, etc.

AMERICAN FOLK SONG

WHAT SHALL WE DO WHEN WE ALL GO OUT, ALL GO OUT, ALL GO OUT,

WHAT SHALL WE DO WHEN WE ALL GO OUT, WHEN WE ALL GO OUT TO PLAY?

Directions: Ask the children to suggest what they might plan to do, such as:

1. We will swing on the swings, on the swings, on the swings.
   We will swing on the swings when we all go out to play.
2. We will climb on the monkey bars, etc.
3. We will slide down the sliding board, etc.
4. We will crawl through the tunnels, etc.
5. We will plant in our garden, etc.
6. We will look for acorns, etc.

As you sing about each activity, the whole group makes an appropriate motion. It is fun to see different interpretations of climbing, sliding, etc.

Variations:

1: "What Shall We Do When We *Can't* Go Out?" Try this version on a rainy or icy cold winter day. The children must pantomine the motions such as:

   We will build with the great big blocks, great big blocks, great big blocks, etc., or:

We will cut and paste today, paste today, paste today, etc., or, actually do these types of motions:

We will roll on the floor today, floor today, floor today, etc.

We will play on our tambourines, tambourines, tambourines, etc., or any other instruments.

2: Use the song for dramatic play such as:
Let's all pretend to be giants, giants, etc.
Let's all pretend to be little mice, little mice, etc.
Let's all pretend to be kangaroos, kangaroos, etc.
Let's all pretend to be snowflakes, snowflakes, etc.

LET'S ALL PRETEND TO BE KANGAROOS

Comments: This is another popular American folk tune whose very simplicity lends itself to any set of words you want to substitute. Try using it for some of those clumsy transition times.

RING AROUND THE ROSY

Age: 3–6 years

Benefits: Body awareness
Concentration skills
Practice in responding to
visual clues

Materials: 8 pieces of poster paper, 8½ × 11″ with a different stick figure on each one

Directions: Sing the song, "Ring Around the Rosy" (move freely around the room while singing). On the last line of the song, substitute "We all do this," for "We all fall down." At the same time the children are singing "We all do this," the teacher holds up a picture of a pose (see illustration) that the children will then assume. Children can take turns holding up the picture.

Comments: Instead of pictures, the teacher or one of the students could make a "statue" pose and the children could imitate that pose.

Section C: Circle Games

Circle games are generally easy to teach, and easy for children to learn. Usually the rhythm is simple and strong. The skills of one circle game often apply to many other circle games. Because children often hold hands and follow a rather prescribed path of movement, there are few chances for error or breakdown.

Circle games have been popular in Western culture for hundreds of years. Perhaps it is because, as children stand close together, watch each other, and function as a single unit, group cohesiveness is the natural outcome.

BLUE BIRD

Age: 2½–5 years

Benefits: Coordinating words and actions
Social skills such as following simple rules, taking turns, stopping
   and starting, picking a partner
Space awareness by following a specific route

Materials: Chairs for each child are arranged in a circle. The spaces between
the chairs are the "windows."

Directions:

1. Eight or more children arrange their chairs in a circle and stand in
front of them. Child 1 is the Blue Bird who starts outside the child-and-
chair circle, weaves in and out the "windows," and sings the following
verse:

2. On the word "tired," the Blue Bird (Child 1) stops behind one of the children, and places his/her hands lightly on the chosen one's shoulders. He/she taps the shoulders, while everyone sings:

3. After singing the tapping verse, the child who has just been tapped becomes a Blue Bird, and now two Blue Birds go in and out the windows as the song is repeated. They finally stop behind two children and tap. Next, four Blue Birds weave in and out, in a line, between the windows (chairs), stop and tap, until all the children have joined the line of Blue Birds, and all weave in and out the windows (the windows are empty chairs).

BOW BELINDA

Age: 5–8 years

Benefits: Development of the social skills of working with a partner and taking turns
Practice in following directions
Development of balance and coordination
Coordination of words and actions

BOW , BOW , BOW BE-LIN-DA BOW . BOW , BOW BE-LIN-DA .

BOW , BOW , BOW BE-LIN-DA, WON'T YOU BE MY PART-NER ?

Verses:

2. Right hand out, Oh Belinda,
   Right hand out, Oh Belinda,
   Right hand out, Oh Belinda,
   Right hand out and shake, shake, shake.

3. Left hand out, Oh Belinda,
   Left hand out, Oh Belinda,
   Left hand out, Oh Belinda,
   Left hand out and shake, shake, shake.

4. Both hands out, Oh Belinda,
   Both hands out, Oh Belinda,
   Both hands out, Oh Belinda,
   Both hands out and shake, shake, shake.

5. Circle round, Oh Belinda,
   Circle round, Oh Belinda,
   Circle round, Oh Belinda,
   Won't you be my darling?

Directions: Double circle, partners facing each other (one partner has his or her back to the circle). Follow the directions in the words of the song. This is a simple version of the game that is easy to do with 5 year old children.

Variation: In the primary grades, the reel-like formation is more appropriate. Form two lines facing each other, about six feet apart. Partners are standing across from each other.

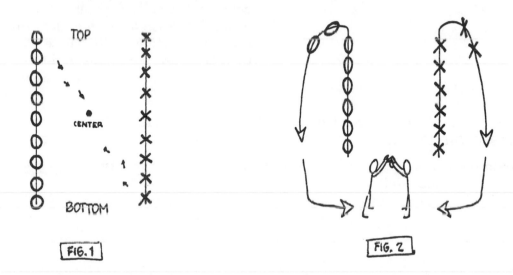

1. Bow, Bow, Bow, Belinda,
   Bow, Bow, Bow, Belinda,
   Bow, Bow, Bow, Belinda,
   Won't you be my partner?

2. Right hand out, Oh, Belinda,
   Right hand out, Oh, Belinda,
   Right hand out, Oh, Belinda,
   Won't you be my partner?

3. Left hand out, Oh, Belinda,
   Left hand out, Oh, Belinda,
   Left hand out, Oh, Belinda,
   Won't you be my partner?

1. Top O and Bottom X advance 3 steps toward the center, bow, take 4 steps back to his or her place. (See Figure 1.) Top X and Bottom O do the same.

2. Top O and Bottom X advance, join right hands, turn in place, and retire. Top X and Bottom O do the same.

3. As above, but with left hands.

4. Both hands out, Oh, Belinda,
   Both hands out, Oh, Belinda,
   Both hands out, Oh, Belinda,
   Won't you be my partner?

5. Shake that big foot, Oh, Belinda,
   Shake that big foot, Oh, Belinda,
   Shake that big foot, Oh, Belinda,
   Won't you be my partner?

6. Promenade all, Oh, Belinda,
   Promenade all, Oh, Belinda,
   Promenade all, Oh, Belinda,
   Won't you be my partner?

4. Same directions as with right and left hands, only use both hands this time.

5. Top O and Bottom X, with arms crossed on chests, advance, go around each other back to back, then retire. The other couple repeats the action. (See Figure 2.)

6. Top O turns to left and leads his/her line around to bottom where he/she meets top X (who has led his/her line around to the right and down to the bottom). When Top O and Top X meet, they form an arch under which the other partners pass. There will then be a new top couple and the former ones remain at the bottom of the lines.

Repeat until all couples have been at the top. With young children, use a skipping step throughout.

Comments: This is a simple introduction to one of our country's most popular old dances.

ROCK CANDY

Age: 3–6 years

For: Body awareness, imitation of movement
Quick thinking, both to imitate what the leader does, and to quickly
think up a motion for others to imitate
Rhythmic use of words in a complete sentence
(On a rainy day, this game can be the source of some vigorous indoor
exercise.)

Directions:

1. Children stand in a circle; one child stands in the center and performs some simple motion or stunt such as a jumping jack. Everyone sings:

ROCK CAN-DY EV-ERY DAY. ROCK CAN-DY EV-ERY DAY.

ROCK CAN-DY EV-ERY DAY, DO YOUR OWN ROCK CAN-DY.

2. Now all the children imitate the one in the center and sing to the same tune:

We can do it, yes we can,
We can do it, yes we can,
We can do it, yes we can,
Do your own rock candy!

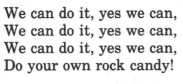

WE CAN DO IT YES WE CAN   WE CAN DO IT YES WE CAN

WE CAN DO IT YES WE CAN   DO YOUR OWN ROCK CAN-DY

FAIR ROSA

Age: 4½ years–first grade

For: Organizing a well-known story into a sequence of verses, each with an action that moves the story along
Social skills, such as taking turns being the main actors; giving and accepting the attention of the group. (Allows a few children to be "the stars" briefly.)
Thinking ahead and preparing to match actions to words

Materials: A stick for a wand, a ruler for a sword, and a chair for a tower are helpful, but not necessary.

Directions: A small group of children (8–12) starts by holding hands and forming a circle. Whoever plays the bad fairy and the prince must wait to one side. Rosa stands in the center near a chair (her tower). All the other children are trees.

See further directions accompanying the other verses.

1. Fair Rosa was a lovely child, lovely child, lovely child. (Circle moves
   Fair Rosa was a lovely child, lovely child.   to the right.)

2. Fair Rosa lived in a great high tower, etc. (Rosa stands on a chair or table.)

3. A fairy came and waved her hand, etc. (Bad fairy is menacing as she waves her wand.)

4. Fair Rosa slept for one hundred years, etc. (Rosa sleeps in the center of the circle, on the floor.)

5. A great big forest grew all around, etc. (Trees start from a stooping position and grow tall.)

6. A galloping prince came riding by, etc. (Prince rides around outside of circle.)

7. He took his sword and cut the trees. (Trees fall down.)

8. He took that Rosa and galloped away, etc. (Prince takes Rosa by the hand and gallops away.)

9. The prince and Rosa lived happily, happily, etc.

Comments: Children love to play this game. However, some teachers may not like this story as it *is* somewhat sexist. Rosa is passive and must be rescued by a competent, dashing prince. Creative teachers might want to reverse the roles: a boy could come under an evil spell, and a competent, dashing princess could help him escape.

OLD BRASS WAGON

Age: 5 years—elementary grades

Benefits: Practice in following directions
           Awareness of left and right movements
           Coordination of actions and words
           Practice in working with a partner

Materials: None for original use of the activity
           Hula-Hoops or a parachute can be used in variations.

CIR-CLE TO THE LEFT, OLD BRASS WA-GON, CIR-CLE TO THE LEFT, OLD BRASS WA-GON.

CIR-CLE TO THE LEFT, OLD BRASS WA-GON, YOU'RE THE ONE MY DAR-LING.

Verses:

2. Circle to the right, Old Brass Wagon.
    Circle to the right, Old Brass Wagon.
    Circle to the right, Old Brass Wagon.
    You're the one, my darling.

3. Swing, oh swing, Old Brass Wagon, etc.
4. Promenade home, Old Brass Wagon, etc.

Directions: Single circle of couples.

1. During the first verse, all join hands and circle to the left.
2. During the second verse, reverse direction and all circle right.
3. During the third verse, swing your partner with a two-hand hold.
4. During the fourth verse, partners promenade (walk) around the circle counter-clockwise (to the right again!), holding inside hands.

Variation: Try using a small group of children around a Hula-Hoop to get the feeling of left and right movement. Keep both hands on at first and *slide* either left or right. Then try switching hands and walking, tiptoeing, or running in either direction.

This same kind of activity can be adapted for use with a parachute and a large group of children.

Adding verses by making up your words is a wonderful way to expand the use of this play party song. The verses can include movement or stand-still actions such as:

Back to back, Old Brass Wagon,
(Do-si-do in square dance terms)
Back to back, Old Brass Wagon,
Back to back, Old Brass Wagon,
You're the one my darling.

or

Flap your wings, Old Brass Wagon,
(Make like a bird!)
Flap your wings, Old Brass Wagon,
Flap your wings, Old Brass Wagon,
You're the one, my darling.

Comments: The tune and words exist in many variations. Since it is easy to sing, both actions and singing can be taught simultaneously.

OL' KING GLORY

Ages: 5–8-years

Benefits: Practice in following directions
Coordination of actions and words

Directions: Single circle facing left. One child is chosen as leader and he/she stands outside the circle. When you start the song, the circle marches around to the left and the leader marches around the outside to the right. At the words "the first one, the second one, the third follow me," the leader taps three children on the head. The third child follows the leader and, the next time, he/she does the tapping. The circle will get smaller and smaller, as more and more children fall out of the circle to follow the leader in the outer circle. The game is repeated until all but one child remains. He/she, of course, is Ol' King Glory! Sing and clap one more verse to "honor" him/her.

OL' KING GLO-RY OF THE MOUN-TAIN, THE MOUN-TAIN WAS SO HIGH, IT

NEAR-LY REACHED THE SKY; THE FIRST ONE, THE SECOND ONE, THE THIRD FOL'LOW ME.

(THE LAST PERSON LEFT IS "OL' KING GLORY")

Variations:

1. Players can stand in a circle and clap the beat, while the leader and his chosen followers continue to march around the outside until everyone is chosen.

2. Change "Ol' King Glory" to "Great Big Giant in the Castle" or "Mean Old Witch on the Mountain."

Comments: A playground game that even older children love to play.

RIG-A-JIG-JIG

Age: 2½–5 years

Benefits: Extension of attention span, listening for signals
Quick changes between fast and slow, loud and soft, walk and run
Social skills like following simple rules, waiting for a turn

Materials: None, but a masking tape circle on the floor helps young children keep their circle round.

Directions:

1. A small group of children (six to eight persons) stands in a circle. If the whole class wants to play, have two or more small groups in circles.

2. The group sings the following verse, very softly, while the first child walks slowly around the circle, looking for a partner.

ENGLISH FOLK SONG

AS JILL WAS WALKING DOWN THE STREET, DOWN THE STREET, DOWN THE STREET; A

FRIEND OF HERS SHE CHANCED TO MEET. HI HO, HI HO, HI HO ——.

CHORUS:

RIG-A-JIG-JIG AND A-WAY WE GO, A-WAY WE GO, A-WAY WE GO,

RIG-A-JIG-JIG AND A-WAY WE GO, HI HO, HI HO, HI HO.

3. Child 1 taps a friend on the shoulder. Suddenly the walk changes to a run, and the singing becomes loud and fast as the group breaks into the Chorus. The two children run around the circle and Child 1 goes into the empty space in the circle.

4. Child 2 walks alone around the now quiet circle, and the song repeats.

Comments: This is a very easy, non competitive circle game. Its lively running action makes it a good indoor activity. Keep the group small so there will be no long waits for turns, or else have more than one circle going at one time.

RIG-A-JIG-JIG AND A-WAY WE GO.

RISE, SUGAR, RISE

Age: 3–5 years

Benefits: Practice in the social skills involved in a simple follow-the-leader game such as the following:

> think up a simple stunt
> sharpen reactions
> wait for a turn to be a leader

The child will observe the various leaders' stunts, and match her/his motions to theirs (promotes body awareness).

Directions: Children stand in a circle, except for Child 1, who stands in the center. This child will be the leader. As the group sings the song, Child 1 will make some simple motion with the arms, legs and/or body, and all the children copy the leader. At the end of the verse, Child 1 picks a new leader and returns to the circle.

MAKE A NIF-TY MO-TION, MA-RIE. MAKE A NIF-TY MO-TION, MA-RIE.

MAKE A NIF-TY MO-TION, MA-RIE. RISE, SU-GAR, RISE.

Comments: Motions should be uncomplicated, so other children can catch on quickly and start to follow the leader promptly.

SHAKE THEM 'SIMMONS DOWN

Age: 5–8 years

Benefits: Practice in following directions
Awareness of left and right movements
Development of coordination and balance
Practice in working with a partner

AMERICAN PLAY PARTY

SHAKE THAT TREE, DO, OH, DO; SHAKE THAT TREE DO, OH, DO;

SHAKE THAT TREE, DO, OH, DO. SHAKE THEM 'SIM-MONS DOWN.

Verses:

2. Right hand crossed, do, oh, do, etc.
3. Left hand crossed, do, oh, do, etc.
4. Swing to the right, do, oh, do, etc.
5. Swing to the left, do, oh, do, etc.
6. All promenade, do, oh, do, etc.

VERSE 1.

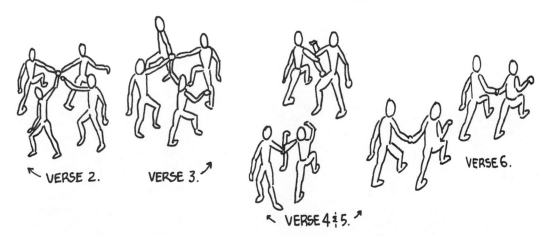

VERSE 2.   VERSE 3.   VERSE 4 & 5.   VERSE 6.

Directions: Circles about the room formed by two sets of partners joining hands to form rings.

1. Circles turn in a counter-clockwise direction, with a light, walking step.
2. Partners take right hands across (like spokes in a wheel) and all proceed in a clockwise direction with the same light walking step.
3. Partners take left hands across and all proceed in a counter-clockwise direction.
4. Partners swing with a right elbow swing.
5. Partners swing with a left elbow swing.
6. Partners take the inside hands and walk around the circle in a counter-clockwise direction. (This could be the entire group—just keep repeating this verse until everyone has joined the big circle.)

Variation: Number each ring of four partners (one, two) and (three, four). When you repeat the dance, have the odd numbers change places with odd numbers in other rings. In the next repetition, have the even numbers change places with even numbers in other rings.

Comments: This is beautiful to watch and the children love the star pattern movement of Verses 2 and 3.

"Simmons" is an abbreviation of persimmons, the plum-like fruit of the persimmon tree.

SHOO FLY

Age: 6–8 years

Benefits: Practice in following directions
Development of quick reactions
Coordination of actions and words
Social give and take

AMERICAN SINGING GAME

SHOO FLY, DON'T BO-THER ME. SHOO FLY, DON'T BO-THER ME.
SHOO FLY, DON'T BO-THER ME; FOR I BE-LONG TO SOME-BO-DY. I
FEEL, I FEEL, I FEEL, I FEEL LIKE A MOR-NING STAR. I
FEEL, I FEEL, I FEEL, I FEEL LIKE A MORN-ING STAR.

Directions: Form a single circle, with or without partners.

1. With all hands joined, everyone walks four steps to the center.
2. All walk four steps back to place.
3. Same as 1.
4. Same as 2.
5–8. Each person turns to somebody near them and swings him/her four times around with a two-hand hold.

Repeat from the beginning, only this time on lines 5–8, ask everyone to turn in the other direction and swing someone else.

Variations:

1: When partners are available, on Lines 5–8, each boy joins both hands with his partner (who is on his right hand side), and swings three-and-a-half times around with her. He leaves his original partner on his left side and begins the dance again with the new girl on his right.

2: On lines 5–8, the circle may be turned inside out. When this is done with a large group, it may be necessary to keep repeating the second half of the song. One couple lifts inside hands to form an arch, while a couple on the opposite side of the circle approaches, leading all the dancers under the arch until the circle is inside out. When all have passed through, the couple forming the arch turns in under their arched arms. After the circle is inside out, the first part of the song is repeated, with everybody backing into the center and out two times. One lines 5–8, the circle can be turned right-side out again by reversing the roles of the two couples who helped turn it inside out: the couple who formed the arch the first time backs across the circle, leading the dancers under an arch now formed by the other couple.

Comments: This is a Play-Party Game dating back to the American Civil War.

SOMEBODY WAITING FOR ME

Age: 5–8 years. (See also "Comments," for a simple variation.)

Benefits: Practice in following directions
Awareness of rhythmic beat
Development of differentiation between left and right and the ability
to reverse
Locomotor movements of skipping and swinging

Directions: Hands are joined in a single circle without partners. One person stands in the middle.

1. The circle walks to the left while the center person walks to the right on the inside of the circle. (16 steps, pivoting on 16.)

2. All reverse direction, the outside circle moving to the right, the inside person moving to the left. (16 steps.)

3. On the first line of this verse, the outside circle faces in, and the center player chooses two people standing next to each other in the circle. He draws them into the center and swings with them while the outside circle stands and claps.

4. The original center person then swings one of the two he has chosen with a two-hand hold and, on the last line of the verse, leads the partner back to the larger circle. The extra person remains in the center to start the dance again.

Comments: This is an American-Play Party Game, so called because anything called "dancing" was sinful.

It's easy to teach, and can be taught as you sing it.

For kindergarten-age children, simplify the directions as follows: walk only in one direction for Verses 1 and 2; let the center person skip around the inside circle until Verse 3.

TZENA-TZENA

Age: 6–10 years

Benefits: Development of coordination (A certain simple rhythmic precision is required to perform the dance.)
Encourages trust and togetherness in groups
Stimulates interest in other cultures. (This is an Israeli dance.)

Directions: *Tzena-Tzena* is a song and dance of celebration that appeals to children because of its gaiety and brisk tempo. The children should be very familiar with the song before attempting the dance. A simple clapping pattern can be used when teaching the song. It will help establish the pattern of the dance-step used later on.

Directions for Dance: Children stand in a very tight circle, with their arms on each other's shoulders. As the music begins, the circle will move counter-clockwise in the following manner: (begin *very* slowly)

|| STEP · STEP · STEP · STEP | HOP · HOP ||

This pattern is repeated again and again as the song is sung. With each verse, the tempo should be quickened until the group simply can't go any faster. End the last, fastest chorus with a huge HUR-RAH!

Variations:

1: More complicated step: everything remains the same with the circle moving counter-clockwise, but begin the dance step with the left foot.

This version requires that the left foot steps over the right, right steps from behind the left, then left step behind the right, right step over the left. The upper body will always face the center circle, rather than turning when stepping in the usual manner. (See illustration below.)

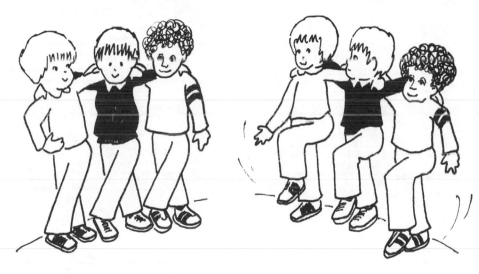

ILLUSTRATING THE LEFT STEPPING
OVER THE RIGHT

THE "HOP":
KNEE HELD UP WHILE HOPPING ON OTHER FOOT.

2: The song can be sung as a round, with Part A being sung against Part B. (Parts A and B are marked in the music.)

Comments: The group will have to "pull" together to perform the dance quickly. With all standing shoulder to shoulder, if one person goofs, the whole circle can fall apart. The complicated step is challenging and worth the extra time it takes to practice.

WILD BIRD

Age: 4–8 years

Benefits: Social skills such as taking turns
Auditory discrimination such as identifying a person by his/her voice

Materials: None (instruments provide variation)

Directions: Children sit in a circle. Child who is "It" sits in the center and covers his/her eyes. The teacher picks another child from the circle to be the Wild Bird. The group sings the song as Wild Bird flies around the inside of the circle. Just before the last phrase of the song ("If you guess my name, you can fly away"), the group stops singing and Wild Bird alone sings the ending phrase ("If you guess my name, etc.") "It" tries to guess the identity of Wild Bird. If correct, "It" goes free and Wild Bird becomes "It," or else two new children can play the two roles.

JAPANESE SINGING GAME

ROUND, ROUND THE WILD BIRDS FLY. POOR LIT-TLE BIRD IN A

CAGE, DON'T CRY. HIDE YOUR EYES AND SOON YOU'LL BE

WITH THE WILD BIRDS FLYING FREE. WHO'S STAND-ING BACK OF YOU,

CAN YOU SAY? IF YOU GUESS MY NAME, YOU CAN FLY A-WAY.

Variation: Use 3 to 4 rhythm instruments to add beauty to the song, and to develop simple rhythmic skills. Instruments such as the triangle, tambourine, finger cymbals, shaker, autoharp, or dulcimer are suitable. Pass the instruments around the circle with each verse.

Comments: This is an immediately successful activity! First and foremost, it is a beautiful song; in addition, children love the game.

SUPER-BOY
by Pat Stemmler

Age: 2–4 years

Benefits: Group cooperation: taking turns and being the center of attention

Directions: Children sit in a circle. Each child has a turn to pick his/her favorite super-hero (Spiderman, Wonder Woman, Batgirl, etc.) and "fly" around the circle as the song is sung.

I WISH I WAS SU-PER BOY. I WISH I WAS SU-PER BOY, IF

I WAS SU-PER BOY, THEN I COULD FLY, AND HELP SOME PEO-PLE, AS TIME GOES BY.

Variations:

1. Replace "Super-Boy" with whichever super-hero the child has picked, and sing: "I wish I was Spider-Man," etc.

2. To use the song as a group activity, have all of the boys "fly" outside the circle on the "Super-Boy" verse; then sing, "I wish I were a Super-Girl," and have all of the girls "fly" around the circle.

Comments: Young children are fascinated with super-hero figures and this simple song absolutely captivates them! Even after playing and singing this song for two years, I have children who repeatedly ask to "sing it again." With 2- to 4-year-olds, it ranks amongst the most popular of any of the songs we sing.

Section D: Camp and Folk Songs

Of all of the songs in this book, these are the ones children will probably remember, even into adulthood. They are invariably rich in either broad humor or subtle wit. They appeal to children of all ages, and bind a group together.

They are primarily for fun and recreation, and can be sung while traveling. You may find that some of these songs will help children move smoothly from one activity to another. These songs are easily transferrable; children will sing them at home, on the playground, and while going about their day.

AIKEN DRUM

Age: 3–7 years

Benefits: Vocabulary development; identification of body parts
Development of memory and ability to concentrate
Collaboration of group members

Materials: Space and implements for simple drawing (a chalkboard or easel, or a large paper taped on a wall, with crayons or chalk for drawing)

Simple rhythm instruments may be used to accompany the Chorus and Variation 1)

Introduction: *(sung at the beginning only)*

THERE WAS A MAN LIVED IN THE MOON, IN THE MOON, IN THE MOON. THERE WAS A MAN LIVED IN THE MOON, AND HIS NAME WAS AI-KEN DRUM.

CHORUS:

AND HE PLAYED UP-ON HIS LA-DLE, HIS LA-DLE, HIS LA-DLE, HE PLAYED UP-ON HIS LA-DLE, AND HIS NAME WAS AI-KEN DRUM.

Verses:

1: His head was made of an _____ . An _____ , an _____ .
His head was made of an _____ , and his name was Aiken Drum.

2: His body was made of a _____ . A _____ , a _____ ,
his body was made of a _____ , and his name was Aiken Drum.

Directions:

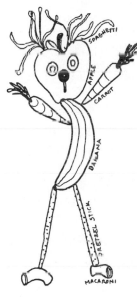

1. Have children sit in a group. Explain that *Aiken Drum* is a silly song about a man who is made out of food . . . and that, as the song is sung, you will draw a picture of Aiken Drum using their ideas for what kind of food to draw.

2. Sing the introduction, then go right onto the Chorus, asking children to clap their hands to make the sound of Aiken's Ladle.

3. At the end of the Chorus, pause long enough to ask the children: "What kind of food would you like to use for Aiken's head?" Call on one child for an idea, accepting any suggestion as long as it is edible! Sing the verse: "His head was made of an _____," drawing the picture of that food as you sing, then sing the Chorus with all clapping hands.

4. Continue in this manner for all the body parts: torso, arms, legs, feet, hands, eyes, hair, etc., soliciting each child's ideas, and always singing and clapping the Chorus at the end of each verse.

5. At the end of the song (when Aiken is complete and/or every child has had a turn to contribute an idea), go over the picture, identifying all of the food and trying to remember whose idea each was. Hang your picture of Aiken Drum in a prominent place.

Variations:

1. Use rhythm instruments (or pots and pans) in place of clapping hands in the Chorus. Use *only* on the chorus when Aiken is playing his ladle.

2. With older children (5–7), be more specific about types of food—ask for vegetables, or draw an Aiken made of fruit; even with young children, you can be more specific: "What kind of food did you eat for breakfast this morning?" "Are there special kinds of foods you eat at Thanksgiving; Passover; etc.?"

3. Five- to seven-year-olds will enjoy drawing their own ideas as you sing the song. The group may work on one collective picture, or each child can draw his or her own.

Comments: This song is always a hit, and stimulates a lot of classroom talk and activity about food.

THE ANTS GO MARCHING

Age: 4–8 years

Benefits: Group solidarity, humor
Counting, acting out numbers

Directions: Children can sing this song anywhere: seated at a table, in a car or van, or at group time. Perhaps the best way to sing it is to have children also walk or crawl across the room in twos, threes, fours or fives (just as the ants do in the song). Or, children may pantomime the actions of "the littlest ant" who ties his/her shoe, picks up sticks, slams the gate or scratches his/her thigh.

Verses:

2. Two by two, the little one stopped to tie his shoe;

3. Three by three, the little one stopped to climb a tree;

4. Four by four, the little one stopped to shut the door;

5. Five by five, the little one stopped to scratch his thigh;

6. Six by six, the little one stopped to pick up sticks;

7. Seven by seven, the little one stopped to go to heaven;

8. Eight by eight, the little one stopped to slam the gate;

9. Nine by nine, the little one said, "I'm behind";

10. Ten by ten, the little one said, "This is the end."

Comments: This is one of those catchy songs that children sing to themselves as they work or play, or sing spontaneously in a small group.

CHICKEN SOUP
by Pat Stemmler

Age: 3–7 years

Benefits: Socialization, relaxation and humor

Directions: This is a good, old-fashioned singing and swaying song, with a little humor added to spice it up. I often hear kids singing or humming it in the hallway, bathroom or outside as they play.

CHICKEN SOUP

Pat Stemmler

I LOVE CHICK-EN SOUP. I LOVE CHICK-EN SOUP. I LOVE TO

SQUISH THOSE NOO-DLES ON THE FLOOR, AND THEN I ASK FOR MORE. 'CAUSE

MAK-IN' CHICK-EN SOUP IS SO MUCH FUN. YOU TAKE SOME

CHICK-EN AND SOME NOO-DLES AND A BIG ON-ION; AND THEN YOU

PUT IT ALL IN A GREAT BIG POT, AND YOU FILL IT WITH WA-TER AND

LET IT GET HOT; AND THEN YOU COOK IT, AND YOU SIM-MER IT

ALL DAY LONG; UN-TIL YOU'RE REA-DY TO SING THIS SONG; AND YOU

SAY "HEY MOM, WOW! I'M REALLY HUN-GRY, I WANT MY CHICKEN SOUP NOW, CAUSE ...

CUMBAYA

Age: 3–8 years

Benefits: Coordination of words with "signs"
Awareness of gestures as language

Directions: There are "signs" for all of the words/phrases of Cumbaya. Begin by teaching the sign for the title. On the first two syllables, *"CUM-BA,"* have the children rotate their hands in front of them in a rolling motion, then gently thrust their hands outward, palms up on the last syllable: *"YA."* (All signs are illustrated on the following page.) After practicing the Cumbaya sign several times, sing the song instructing the children to perform the sign whenever they hear the word, "Cumbaya" sung.

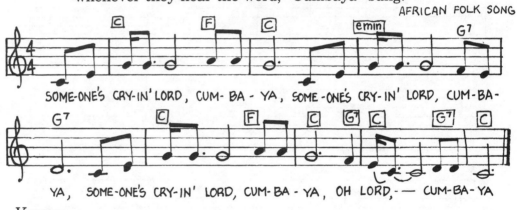

AFRICAN FOLK SONG

SOME-ONE'S CRY-IN' LORD, CUM-BA-YA, SOME-ONE'S CRY-IN' LORD, CUM-BA-YA, SOME-ONE'S CRY-IN' LORD, CUM-BA-YA, OH LORD,—CUM-BA-YA

Verses:

1. Someone's cryin' Lord, Cumbaya
   Someone's cryin' Lord, Cumbaya
   Someone's cryin' Lord, Cumbaya
   Oh Lord, Cumbaya.

CRYING

2. Someone's prayin' Lord, Cumbaya
   Someone's prayin' Lord, Cumbaya
   Someone's prayin' Lord, Cumbaya
   Oh Lord, Cumbaya.

PRAYING

SMILING

3. Someone's smilin' Lord, Cumbaya
   Someone's smilin' Lord, Cumbaya
   Someone's smilin' Lord, Cumbaya
   Oh Lord, Cumbaya.

4. Someone's singin' Lord, Cumbaya
   Someone's singin' Lord, Cumbaya
   Someone's singin' Lord, Cumbaya
   Oh Lord, Cumbaya.

SINGING

CUM - BA - : YA

ROTATE HANDS IN A ROLLING MOTION STOPPING ON "YA" WITH PALMS UP.

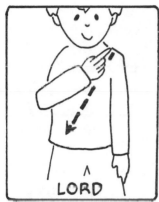

LORD

"DRAW" A LINE ACROSS CHEST

OH

SOME-ONE'S

TOUCH RIGHT ELBOW ON "SOME"
TOUCH LEFT ELBOW ON "ONES"

Hints: Pre-school children: singing and signing *cumbaya* is challenging enough. Add other signs gradually, *after* the song is well-known by all the children. Introduce new signs in this order: 1. Cumbaya, 2. Lord, 3. Oh, 4. Someone's.

First graders and older can usually learn all signs and the song simultaneously. Stand before the group and model all the signs as the song is sung; by Verse 4, the kids will have it!

Variation: All ages: when the complete sign language and song have been learned, it is fun (and valuable) to conclude the song with a verse that is hummed and signed. It's even more challenging to finish in total silence, "singing" the song only with the hands.

Comments: This beautiful and popular song has been recorded by many folksingers. After the children have been singing it themselves, they will enjoy having you play one of these recordings for them.

"Cumbaya" is "Pidgin English" for "come by here."

HUSH LITTLE BABY

Age: 3 through elementary grades

Benefits: Language development (especially rhyming words)
Development of auditory memory, such as remembering the rhyming word and the sound to carry over to the next phrase
Development of auditory discrimination, as in comparing the sounds of two words for rhyming qualities

HUSH LIT-TLE BA-BY, DON'T SAY A WORD.

MA-MA'S GOING TO BUY YOU A MOCK-ING BIRD.

Verses:

2. If that mocking bird won't sing,
   Mama's going to buy you a diamond ring.

3. If that diamond ring turns brass,
   Mama's going to buy you a looking glass.

4. If that looking glass gets broke,
   Mama's going to buy you a billy goat.

5. If that billy goat gets bony,
   Mama's going to buy you a Shetland pony.

6. If that pony runs away,
   Mama's going to buy you another some day.

Directions: When you are teaching the song, leave out the last two words of each verse and let the children fill them in. Call attention to the rhyming words. Sometimes in the folk song versions the rhymes are not always perfect!

Variation: I never got by with just the "Mama" version. We always had to do it over with "Papa's going to buy...."

With little children, the teacher could pose another "If" situation and let the children suggest the rhyming solution. With older children, have them make up the entire additional verses. Think of a good ending like:

> If that pony won't be led,
> We're all so tired, we're going to bed!

Comments: Who doesn't know this song?

I HAVE A CAR

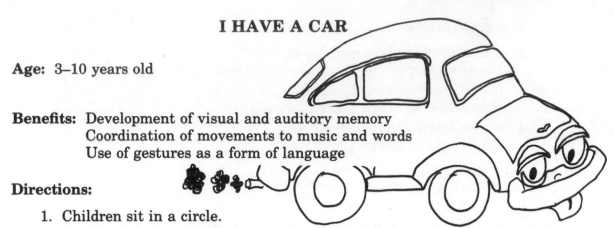

Age: 3–10 years old

Benefits: Development of visual and auditory memory
Coordination of movements to music and words
Use of gestures as a form of language

Directions:

1. Children sit in a circle.
2. First teach the ostinato pattern (see below) using both words and movements. Have children "echo" the words and mimic your movements.

Ostinato Pattern

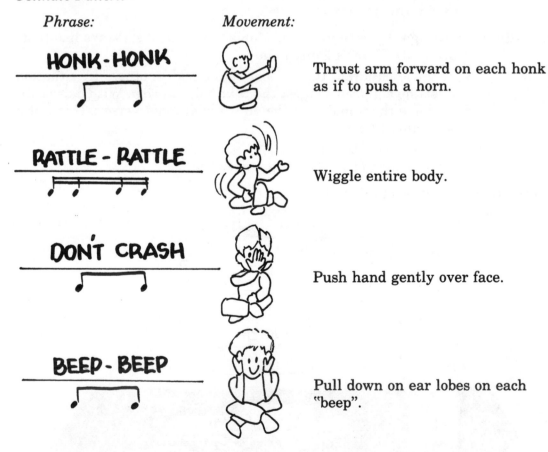

Phrase:	*Movement:*
HONK-HONK	Thrust arm forward on each honk as if to push a horn.
RATTLE-RATTLE	Wiggle entire body.
DON'T CRASH	Push hand gently over face.
BEEP-BEEP	Pull down on ear lobes on each "beep".

3. After you have practiced the ostinato pattern a couple of times, begin singing the song slowly, again using motions as you sing.

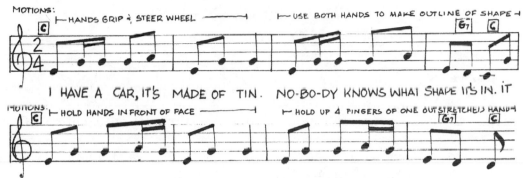

I HAVE A CAR, IT'S MADE OF TIN. NO-BO-DY KNOWS WHAT SHAPE IT'S IN. IT

HAS A MIRROR AND A RUN-NING BOARD; IT'S A FORD AND IT HAS FOUR DOORS.

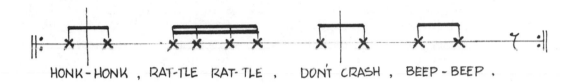

HONK-HONK, RAT-TLE RAT-TLE, DON'T CRASH, BEEP-BEEP.

4. Continue to sing the song over and over, getting just a bit faster each time. By the sixth time through, you will be singing and chanting the ostinato so quickly that it should be nearly impossible, and very funny.

Variations:

1. For older children (7–10 years). divide the group in half. Half the group (Group 1) begins the ostinato pattern, while the other group (Group 2) sings the song—(the ostinato is done throughout the song). The groups will come together at the end of the song, both repeating the ostinato pattern twice. Now the singing roles are reversed: Group 1 sings the song as Group 2 performs the ostinato. The pace accelerates with each Chorus, until it is too fast to keep up with.

2. Pick four children from the group and assign each child one phrase of the ostinato. In other words, the first child will chant the "honk-honk"; the second child will chant the "rattle-rattle," the third "don't crash," and so forth. Have them stand in front of the group and be ready to come in on their part. This takes great concentration and even better anticipation.

Comments: This old camp song appeals to children of all ages. They will especially love the silly movements that continue throughout the song and ostinato. Remember to keep the pace quite slow when beginning, especially with the younger children.

I LOVE SCHOOL, YES I DO
by Pat Stemmler

Age: 3–7 years

Benefits: Develops sense of rhythm and meter through anticipation of the "Yes I Do" response
Exploration of feelings about school with the use of humor
Development of sensitivity to others

Directions: Speak the phrase "Yes I do." Have the children echo the phrase. Repeat that phrase again, playing an "echo-ing" game with the group—have children echo your inflection as well. Say it emphatically, with puzzlement, yell it, whisper it, sing it. Now you are ready to sing the song. Instruct the children to listen carefully and to be ready to echo, "Yes I do," when they hear it in the song.

I LOVE SCHOOL, YES I DO (YES I DO). I LOVE SCHOOL, YES I DO (YES I DO). OH
                                    ECHO   ECHO

I LOVE SCHOOL CAUSE I LOVE THOSE SIL-LY RULES, I LOVE SCHOOL YES I DO (YES I DO).
                                                                           ECHO

Before long, some kid will get the idea to say, "No I don't." Be prepared and *look surprised!* Lots of laughter will begin as all the children join in the new "No I don't" (there's nothing like rebellion to put a gleam in a child's eye!). *Astonishment* on your face, you say "you don't like school? There must be *something* about school that you like. AHA! You like to build with blocks—let's put that phrase in the song and everybody who likes to build should say: 'Yes I do' at the right time." Sing: "I like to build with the blocks, Yes I do," and so on.

Comments: This is a light-hearted song that will be silly at first, then get more serious as a discussion of school activities is developed. The teacher should be prepared to accept ideas of the students with an open mind. The most interesting development will be the astonished reactions of one student to another: "You *like* reading?!! Boy, you're crazy."

There are predictable "safe" areas: usually everyone likes recess and lunch, and everyone hates "rest."

THE MAN AND THE GOAT
(A Camp Song)

Age: 6–10 years

Comments: Primarily for fun, this camp song brings home to children the pleasure that can be had through word-play and an outrageous fantasy set to music. Camp songs are great equalizers. Children of all ages immediately fall into the humorous spirit.

There was a man
Now please take note
There was a man,
who had a goat.

He loved that goat,
Indeed he did,
He loved that goat
Just like a kid.

One day that goat,
Felt frisk and fine.
Ate three red shirts
From off the line.

That man he grabbed
Him by the back
And tied him to
The railroad track

And as the train
Pulled into sight
That goat grew pale
And green with fright.

He heaved a sigh,
As if in pain,
Coughed up those shirts
And flagged the train.

Optional chant:

Hey!

Walkin' down the *road* and the *road* was *mud*dy,
Stubbed my *toe* and my *toe* was *bloody,*

Give me *two* pounds of *wash*ing-powder,
Two pounds of *soap,*
Don't give *me* no *hard* way to *go.*

Hey!

I say *Hey, hey, did*dle-ee-*bop*
Your *mama's* got the *measles,* your *daddy* chicken *pox.*

(fading)   *Choo*-choo-choo-choo,
          Choo-choo-choo-choo, etc.

Hint: In order to get the rhythm of the chant, you keep the beat on the itali-
cized words.

NAVAJO HAPPY SONG

Age: 5–8 years

Benefits: Development of locomotor skills—moving to a very strong accented beat.
Group cooperation.
Language development—use of Indian words meaning no more than our TraLaLa.
Use of native instruments to accompany the song.

Materials: None are essential, but the addition of drums, rattles, and bells is not only authentic, but a real plus for this "happy song." Making your own instruments makes this activity a real winner.

Directions: Sing the song through three times, accenting the words marked with a > over the music. Add the last two measures to end the song—shouting the "Yah." Clap the > words to emphasize the strong rhythm needed. Transfer the hand clapping to a drum beat on the accented words.

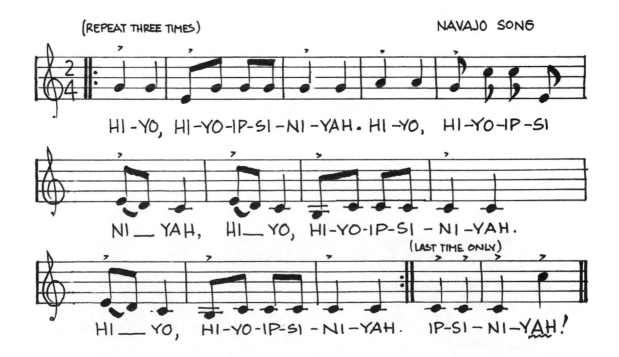

Variations:

1: Add maracas and bells to the accented drum accompaniment. For older children, the rattles and bells could play the accompaniment twice as fast as the drum beat, giving the song more rhythmic variation. It is also easy for some children to beat the rhythm of the words, which gives you yet another rhythmic variation.

2: Add some *simple* movement as you sing. Form a circle in which you could walk around on the accented beats. Everyone faces in when you shout the ending. As you stand on a circle, you could also all face the center and step sideways slowly around the circle on the accented beat. A third movement activity could be a line moving freely in and out all over the room, taking a step on each accented beat.

3: Make your own instruments. Drums can be made out of all sizes of coffee cans or oatmeal boxes. Stretching rubber over the tops gives the best sound, but other things can be used. Rattles can be made out of any simple plastic, tin or waxed carton containers filled with beans or small pebbles. Or you can string items that rattle on a necklace or bracelet. Bells on a bracelet or anklet band are also effective.

Comments: I find that the study of Native Americans (Indians) has as much interest and appeal to teachers as it does to children!

HOMEMADE INSTRUMENTS

DRUM:

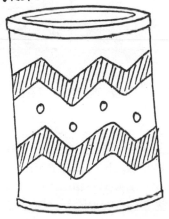

COFFEE, PEANUT OR LEMONADE CANS WITH PLASTIC LIDS : COVER WITH CONSTRUCTION PAPER TO DECORATE OR SPRAY PAINT CAN AND DECORATE WITH COLORED TAPE.

RATTLES:

TWO ALUMINUM PIE PLATES (LARGE OR SMALL) FILLED WITH GRAVEL OR BEANS, STAPLED OR TAPED TO HOLD TOGETHER

MAKE A RATTLE-STICK USING BOTTLE CAPS NAILED TO A ½" DOWEL OR THICK STICK FOUND OUTSIDE. CHILDREN CAN USE TEMPERA PAINT TO DECORATE STICK.

A PEANUT WAS SITTING ON A RAILROAD TRACK
(A Camp Song)

Age: 3–10 years

Benefits: Group solidarity
Humor
(See also "Comments" below.)

Comments: Children find hilarious the fate of a peanut, squashed into peanut butter by a passing train. Before we condemn children for being "gross," remember that incongruities that adults find humorous are often not understood by children. Conversely, young children may require broad or obvious incongruity to get hold of the joke.

This song has no accompanying "action," and is of little redeeming educational value. However, it puts children in a very good humor, perhaps because they have felt "railroaded" or squashed sometimes, or simply because they think this is a strange way to make peanut butter.

THE OLD WOMAN WHO SWALLOWED A FLY

Age: 6–12 years

Benefits: Memory; anticipation of what's coming next
Sequence and organization
Humor and group spirit

Materials: Picture cards, if desired

Directions: This song consists of a series of absurdities that are repeated in a longer and longer chain with each verse. This humorous chain of words is of the same type of humor as "The House That Jack Built."

Younger children will find the "backward sequence" much easier to sing in correct order if the teacher will hold up a row of simple line drawings of the animals as they appear in this song. Or the teacher may put the animal pictures on cards, to be held up in the order of the animals' "appearance."

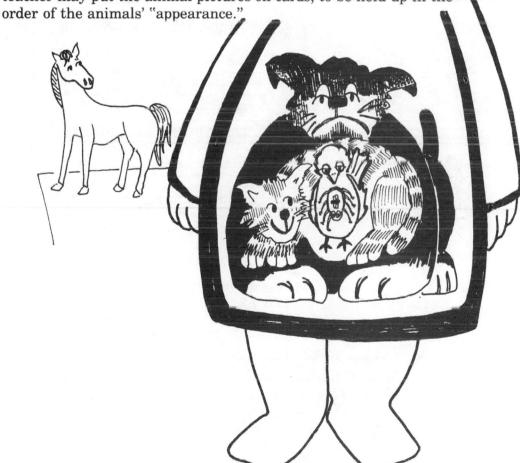

(End each verse with "I don't know why she swallowed the fly.
Perhaps she'll die.")

Verses:

2: I know an old woman who swallowed a bird.
   Wasn't that absurd! She swallowed a bird!
   She swallowed the bird to catch the spider,
   That wiggled and jiggled and tickled inside her.
   She swallowed the spider to catch the fly,
   I don't know why she swallowed the fly.
   Perhaps she'll die.

3: I know an old woman who swallowed a cat.
Imagine that! She swallowed a cat!
She swallowed the cat to catch the bird, etc.
She swallowed the bird to catch the spider,
That wiggled and jiggled and tickled inside her.
She swallowed the spider to catch the fly,
I don't know why she swallowed the fly.
Perhaps she'll die.

4: I know an old woman who swallowed a dog. Wasn't she a hog? She swallowed a dog! etc.

5: I know an old woman who swallowed a goat. Just opened her throat, and swallowed the goat, etc.

Last verse: I know an old woman who swallowed a horse.
(Speak) She's dead! Of course.

ON TOP OF SPAGHETTI
(A Camp Song)

Age: 5–10 years

Benefits: Group enjoyment, humor
Some matching of words with music, sequencing, and auditory memory

TUNE: "ON TOP OF OLD SMOKEY"

ON TOP OF SPA-GHE-TTI ALL CO-VERED WITH CHEESE; I

LOST MY POOR MEAT-BALL, WHEN SOME-BO-DY SNEEZED.

On top of spaghetti, all covered with cheese
I lost my poor meatball, when somebody sneezed.

It rolled off the table, and onto the floor
And then my poor meatball, rolled out of the door.

It rolled in the garden and under a bush
And then my poor meatball was nothing but mush.

The mush was as tasty as tasty could be
And early next summer it grew into a tree.

The tree was all covered with beautiful moss
It grew lovely meatballs and tomato sauce.

So if you eat spaghetti, all covered with cheese
Hold onto your meatballs and don't ever sneeze.

Comments: This is the kind of silly song that appeals to primary children's broad sense of humor. Warning: teachers will tire of it quickly; children, never!

OONIE-KOONIE-CHA

Age: 3–8 years

Benefits: Recognition of beat and sensing changes in tempo
Use of memory in sequence of clapping patterns
Group solidarity: everyone has to work together

Directions: Have group sit in a tight circle with legs crossed; the children's knees should almost be touching. The song will be sung over and over again, with a different and more difficult clapping pattern on each successive verse. (Each clapping pattern is sustained throughout *one* complete verse of the song.)

Younger groups may use a simple clap to begin with, then add on easy patterns such as a knee clap or knee-floor slap as they learn the song and gain confidence.

Older children will be able to string together long sequences of various clapping patterns that will be very challenging to them.

All ages enjoy the challenge of singing each verse faster and faster, trying to keep the claps in tempo with the quickening pace of the voice.

Please Note: There are two parts of the song that depart from the clapping pattern and are *always* done in the same way on every verse:

1. Notice the hold symbol over the first note of the song: the action is to hold both hands high in the air and wiggle all the fingers. The holding of the note acts as a pause between each verse, giving everyone a chance to catch up and get together.

2. For the last two syllables, Kee-Chee should be acted out as follows:

On *"Kee,"* hands are raised with palms down and parallel to the ground at about eye-level.

On *"Chee,"* the forehead is rested on the hands. Children hold this position until the teacher begins singing the "Ah" holding note as a signal for the next verse.

Suggested sequence of clapping patterns:

1. Simple rhythmic clap
2. Alternating clap from the hands to the knees to the hands, etc.
3. Alternating clap from the knees to the floor to the knees, etc.
4. Move from side to center right on the knees (See illustration.)

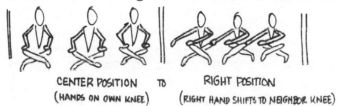

CENTER POSITION   TO   RIGHT POSITION
(HANDS ON OWN KNEE)   (RIGHT HAND SHIFTS TO NEIGHBOR KNEE)

5. Move left from the side to the center on the knees
6. Center to the left side, then to the center to the right side

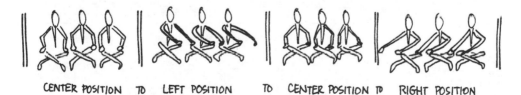

CENTER POSITION   TO   LEFT POSITION   TO   CENTER POSITION TO   RIGHT POSITION

7. In and out movement of both hands in opposite directions

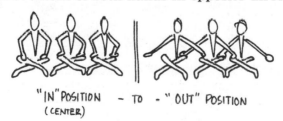

"IN" POSITION   – TO – " OUT" POSITION
(CENTER)

SATURDAY NIGHT

Age: 3–10 years

Benefits: Concentration and attention to the task involved in performing a two-part song or round

Self-concept by the expression of likes and dislikes

Humor and group togetherness

Materials: Rhythm instruments for Variation 2.

Directions: Teach children the rhythm ostinato and have them continue to sing that part as the teacher sings the song.

If the group is unable to "hold" their part, return to practicing the ostinato all by itself. (Preschool children sometimes need the support of an adult singing their part with them.) When the group is able to maintain their ostinato while the teacher sings the song, they should be congratulated and praised on their good work and concentration. Now is the time for them to learn the song. Have the children sing the song with you, then have them try to sing the song while you sing the ostinato. Finally, when they know both parts well, divide the children into two groups and have them perform both parts all by themselves: one group singing the ostinato and the other singing the song.

Variations:

    1: *(Especially for pre-schoolers)* Since the song talks about "Love," have the children think about things that they love (or like) and insert their suggestions into the song. For instance: "Everybody loves chocolate ice cream."

       Someone in the group might also suggest "hating" something; this is another area you might want to explore, again changing the words slightly to accommodate the children's ideas.

    2: Use rhythm instruments to play the ostinato rhythm:

      Pre-School: Divide children into two groups. One group will use the instruments to play *and* sing the ostinato, while the other group sings the song. Then trade places.

      Kindergarten: Classify sounds of the rhythm instruments you have available, dividing them into three groups: wood, metal and skins.

    3: Try having children clap the ostinato (or play it on rhythm instruments) while simultaneously singing the song.

SCARY OLD SKELETON

Age: 3–7 years

Benefits: Development of rhythm and anticipation (sensing when to yell, "BOO").

Use of language skills to make up their own verses

Unusual vocal effects help exploration of the idea of the voice as an instrument

Group fun and solidarity

Materials: Rhythm instruments used in Variation 1

Directions: The song is sung for eight measures, then is followed by four measures of sound effects, with a final, surprising, "BOO!"

VERSE 2.

I AM A SCARY OLD WITCH
I FLY UPON MY BROOM
I FRIGHTEN ALL THE GIRLS AND BOYS
WHEN I PEEK INTO THEIR ROOMS.
(WITCH'S CACKLE FOR 7 BEATS) BOO!

VERSE 3.

I AM A LIT-TLE GHOST
I FLY UP IN THE SKY
I FRIGHT-EN ALL THE GIRLS AND BOYS
WHEN THEY GO RUNNING BY.
(GHOSTLY WHO-0-0's FOR 7 BEATS) ... BOO!

Variations:

1: Use any variety of rhythm instruments for the sound effects section of the song. Suggestions: use the woodblock for skeletons, the slide whistle/kazoo or jingle bells for ghosts and maracas/tambourines for the witch's laugh.

2: Children love to make up their own verses for this song about monsters, black cats, super heroes, etc.

Comments: This is a good Halloween song, but it's popular all year 'round. Kids especially like making unusual vocal sounds and the big "BOO" at the end. The words to Verses 1 and 2 were written by the five-year-old children of Wilson School, St. Louis, Missouri, in about 1973.

SHE'LL BE COMIN' ROUND THE MOUNTAIN

Age: 3–8 years

Benefits: Development of visual and auditory memory
Practice in sequencing words and actions as they accumulate
Coordination of actions and words

Materials: None in the original version
Instrumental or environmental sounds can be substituted in variations.

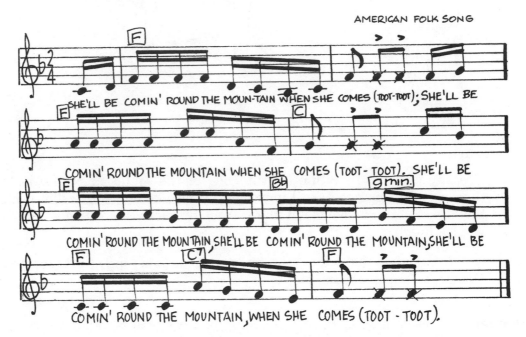

1. She'll be comin' round the mountain, when she comes, Toot, Toot!
   She'll be comin' round the mountain, when she comes, Toot, Toot!
   She'll be comin' round the mountain, She'll be comin' round the mountain,
   She'll be comin' round the mountain when she comes, Toot, Toot! (Pull on chord.)

2. She'll be riding six white horses when she comes, Whoa, Whoa (Pull back on reins.)
   She'll be riding six white horses when she comes, Whoa, Whoa (Pull back on reins.)
   She'll be riding six white horses, she'll be riding six white horses,
   She'll be riding six white horses when she comes, Whoa, Whoa! Toot, Toot!

3. And we'll all go out to meet her when she comes, Hi there! (Wave hand in greeting.)
   And we'll all go out to meet her when she comes, Hi there! (Wave hand in greeting.)
   And we'll all go out to meet her, and we'll all go out to meet her,
   And we'll all go out to meet her when she comes, Hi, there! Whoa, Whoa! Toot-Toot!

4. Then we'll kill that old red rooster when she comes, Chop, Chop! (Chopping motion at neck.)
   Then we'll kill that old red rooster when she comes, Chop, Chop! (Chopping motion at neck.)
   Then we'll kill that old red rooster, then we'll kill that old red rooster,
   Then we'll kill that old red rooster when she comes, Chop, Chop! Hi there! Whoa-Whoa! Toot Toot!

5. And we'll all have chicken and dumplings when she comes, Yum, Yum (Rub tummy.)
   And we'll all have chicken and dumplings when she comes, Yum, Yum (Rub tummy.)
   And we'll all have chicken and dumplings, and we'll all have chicken and dumplings,
   And we'll all have chicken and dumplings when she comes, Yum, Yum! Chop, Chop! Hi there! Whoa-Whoa! Toot, Toot!

Additional verses:

And she'll wear her red pajamas when she comes, Whoo-ee! (Shout or whistle.)

Or, substitute "Scratch, Scratch!" and use a scratching motion to accompany the words.

Then she'll get to sleep with Grandma when she comes, Snore, Snore! (Make a snoring sound.)

Variation: Substitute instrumental sounds for all of the actions and sounds. Act out the whole song as you sing it.

Comments: This is a favorite that keeps cropping up wherever you are.

TRAIN SONG

Age: 3 years through primary grades

Benefits: Language development
Development of locomotor skills such as moving at different speeds, slowing down, speeding up
Imaginative play
Group cooperation

Directions: When you are first introducing this song, children should come in only on the responses, "Oh, yes." The teacher or leader will suggest the one line that is repeated for each verse. Once it is well known, everyone will sooner or later sing everything, and the verses will most likely never be alike twice. It is a song that lends itself to a myriad of different moods.

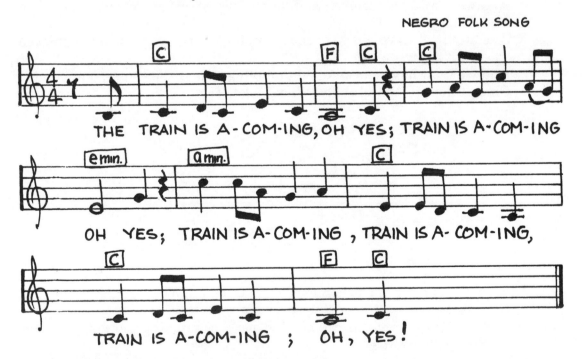

NEGRO FOLK SONG

THE TRAIN IS A-COM-ING, OH YES; TRAIN IS A-COM-ING
OH YES; TRAIN IS A-COM-ING, TRAIN IS A-COM-ING,
TRAIN IS A-COM-ING ; OH, YES!

Suggested Verses:

2. Better get your ticket, Oh, yes!
   Better get your ticket, Oh, yes!
   Better get your ticket, better get your ticket,
   Better get your ticket, Oh, yes!

3. Room for many more, Oh, yes!
4. Hear the whistle blowin'.
5. Hear the conductor callin', "All aboard!"
6. The train is a leavin', Oh, yes!
7. Now the wheels are rollin', Oh, yes!
8. I'm on my way to Texas, Oh, yes!

Variations:

1: Let each child be a different car on a freight or passenger train (engine, coal car, tank car, flat car, caboose, dining car, sleeping car, parlor car, etc.)

Example: Andy is the engine, oh yes. Add movement after all cars are "hitched up." Start up slow and then speed up. Once in a while, there could be a wreck!

2: Let each child be one of the trainmen such as the engineer, the fireman, the brakeman, the conductor, or a passenger. Stop and start the train at different stations to pick up new passengers. This gives lots of practice in changing speeds. Use small shuffling steps and try not to step on your neighbor!

Comments: A train ride to the next activity sure beats "lining up" and passing quietly.

A RUM SUM SUM

Age: 3–8 years

Benefits: Development of rhythmic co-ordination; matching motions to music
Establishment of concepts of tempo and dynamic range such as faster, slower, louder, softer.
Development of concentration and attention to task.

Directions: Have children watch as you demonstrate the song with the motions. Each phrase has its own simple motion that is performed whenever the phrase is sung. (See illustration.) Then, sing the song very slowly and have the children sing and motion with you, going a bit faster with each successive verse.

Variations:

1. Sing the song through 4 or 5 times, getting softer and softer with each verse, until the last verse is done in complete silence with motions.

2. The song can be sung in a round (Parts 1 and 2 are marked above the staff in the music) by 5- through 8-year-old children.

Section E: Follow the Leader and Echo Games

Because they are based on mimicry, these games are very easy to learn. For the same reason, the exact copying of words or movements makes them superb vehicles for listening and observing closely, then following precisely. It must be a relief at times *not* to have to be creative and to just copy what the leader is doing. This is especially true for the very young child who can, as a change of pace, find confidence and security in learning new ideas by rote or repetition.

Echoing a song is not only an easy way to learn, but is also aesthetically pleasing to the ear.

FOOEY
(A Chant)

Age: 3–8 years

Benefits: Build attention and concentration
Social skills (following the leader and taking turns)
Group solidarity

Directions:

1. Children sit in a circle with the teacher.
2. The teacher begins a simple movement pattern, instructing the children to imitate his/her movement, such as (clapping, patting their heads, patting their knees, snapping their fingers).
3. When all the children have joined in the movement, the leader yells "FOOEY!" and changes his/her pattern. All follow by yelling "FOOEY!" and changing the pattern to match that of the leader.
4. Game gets faster and faster, with changes coming more and more quickly.

Variations:

1. When the children clearly understand the format of following and changing, the game can be extended by going from a stationary position to moving all over the room with larger movements, such as jumping, hopping, marching, or running.

2. Four- to five-year-old children will enjoy being the leader for this game.

3. Older children (six to eight years old) might be more challenged by staggering their motions with the leader:

   a) The leader begins a movement, everyone *watches* that movement, but they do not imitate it yet.
   b) Leader yells "FOOEY!" and changes to a new movement. Children *then* yell "FOOEY!" and begin the leader's *first* movement.
   c) Every time the leader changes, the group must also change to the leader's *previous* movement. This becomes difficult as the game gets faster and faster.

Comment: Always remember to yell "FOOEY!"

JOIN IN THE GAME

Age: 3–6 years

Benefits: Coordination of actions and words
Development of body awareness
Attention-span (listening for the exact moment of participation)

Materials: None for the original activity
Small percussion instruments or their substitutes can be used in
an expansion of this activity.

Directions: Substitute other actions and sounds for clapping, such as:

(Roll hands with me.) 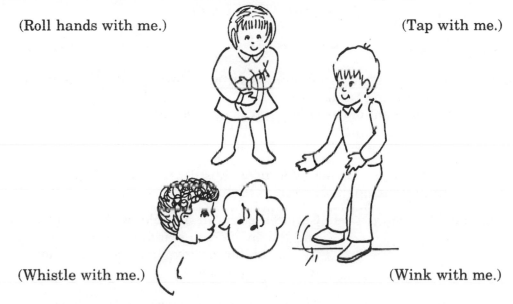 (Tap with me.)

(Whistle with me.) (Wink with me.)

Or, stamping, waving, shaking, clucking, snapping or yawning. The choices are endless!

Variation: You could ask the children to use simple musical instruments to make the sounds, playing only when a certain instrument was called for. This is a good activity for auditory discrimination: that is, comparing the sounds produced by metals, skins and wood. You can even find duplicates of these sounds and others in the classroom if you want to challenge the children in this kind of creative activity. (For example: tapping a metal radiator, tapping two pencils together or tapping your own shoe.)

Comments: This is a good "follow the leader" game song. Once it is well known, children can easily be the leader.

KYE-KYE KOLA *(pronounced key-key cool-a)*
(African Game Chant)

Age: 4–10 years

Benefits: Development of social skills such as following directions and rules, or taking turns
Development of rhythmic coordination such as matching the motions to the chant
Awareness of a sequence of events

Materials: A drum and mallet (You may substitute a pot and spoon, or anything that might be used to keep a beat.)

Directions: *The Chant:*

1. Children stand in a circle, with the "drummer" and the "it" person standing in the center. (Until the children have learned the chant, the teacher should be the drummer.) The drummer begins a beat on the drum. Tell the children to "echo" the drummer's song and movements.

2. The drummer continues the beat and begins the chant, singing each phrase and pausing to allow the children to echo.

3. "It" person leads the movements. The other children should mimic the movement as they echo each phrase. Note that the body position gets lower with each phrase, finally ending in a crouching position on the last phrase.

4. After the chant has been sung, everyone counts to five on the beat of the drum while remaining in a crouch.

Directions: *The Game:*

RUNNING AWAY

1. On the count of "five," all the children may jump up and run away from the circle.

2. "It" runs after everyone and tries to catch somebody by tagging him or her.

3. When "It" does catch another child by tagging, he or she brings the captive back to the approximate center of the circle and the drummer begins the chant.

4. The chant acts as a signal to return to the circle to begin the game again, this time with the two "Its" trying to tag somebody when the game begins.

5. Since the "It" people will double with each successive chant, it won't be long until everyone has been caught.

6. End the game with one last chant, leaving out the count so that everyone remains in the circle.

Variation: After the game has been learned and is very familiar to the children, add another dimension by counting to five in Swahili. (See illustration.)

Comments: I have played this game with large groups of children in very large outdoor spaces and it always amazes me how they dash right back to the circle when they hear the drumbeat and chant begin. It has built-in success for everyone!

By the way, the Swahili phrases of the chant are pronounced phonetically.

MY AUNT CAME BACK

Age: Kindergarten through third grade.

Benefits: Coordination of several simultaneous body movements
Socialization, relaxation and humor
Development of listening skills and "echoing"
Body awareness

Directions: Children generally begin standing in a circle. The leader sings each line, then the group echoes it. When the leader starts a motion such as the cutting motion used with the word "shears," it is continued throughout the song. Each motion is added on to previous ones. This makes for mass hysteria.

TUNE: "HOW DRY I AM"

MY AUNT CAME BACK   ECHO: MY AUNT CAME BACK   FROM OLD AL-GIERS;   ECHO: FROM OLD ALGIERS

AND SHE BROUGHT ME BACK   ECHO: AND SHE BROUGHT ME BACK   A PAIR OF SHEARS.   ECHO: A PAIR OF SHEARS

STOMP RIGHT FOOT

2. My aunt came back
   From Holland too,
   And she brought me back
   a wooden shoe.

FAN SELF WITH HAND

3. My aunt came back
   From old Japan,
   And she brought me back
   A paper fan.

"CHEWING"

4. My aunt came back
   From old Belgium,
   And she brought me back
   Some bubble gum.

ROCK UP AND DOWN

5. My aunt came back
   From the county fair,
   And she brought me back
   A rocking chair.

6. My aunt came back
   From old Chile,
   And she brought me back
   An itchy flea.

7. My aunt came back
   From the city zoo,
   And she brought me back
   A nut like you!

THIS IS WHAT I CAN DO

Age: 3–5 years

Benefits: Social skills such as following a leader's directions, becoming the leader, and taking turns

Thinking skills such as planning ahead while attending to the task at hand

A good game for transition times (See Comments.)

Directions: The group should be seated in a circle. Tell children that this is a follow-the-leader game (and everyone will have a turn as the leader) in which you, the teacher, will think of movements they can imitate with their upper bodies, hands, arms, heads and faces. Any kind of movement is acceptable, as long as it can be done while sitting down. You begin the game, singing the song and performing a simple movement they all should follow. At the end of the song say, "Now I pass it on to you." The leadership passes to the child on the right, and will continue around the circle until everyone has had a turn.

Variation: As you sing the song, insert the name of the child who is leader: "This is what *Johnny* can do . . ." or "This is what *Sarah* can do. . . ."

Comments: This very simple and effective game can be played whenever there is a "free" moment.

Part 2

CHANTS

Chants are just songs without music, rhythmic speech or, you might say, poetic fun. Because there is no music to learn, chants are very easy to teach, and offer all the benefits of rhythmic speech and the coordination of words and movement. You often find that a chant unites and even mesmerizes a group.

A hint for teaching: even though the rhythms of a chant are built into the words, teachers should say the chant over and over to themselves, to become completely familiar with the pattern of words and rhythms, before introducing it to the children.

Section A: Finger Game Chants

Fingergame chants contain almost all the benefits of musical fingergames (Section IA), but are easier to teach and learn.

Each fingergame tells an amusing story, often based on a fantasy. Although children don't think about it, fingergames illustrate the fun to be had without "things", with only an idea and a group with which to share it.

Even though the tasks may seem simple, it sometimes takes time and practice to coordinate all of the words, rhythms and actions. Teachers should not expect every child's fingers to be equally coordinated.

ALI BABA, FORTY THIEVES

Age: 3–5 years

Benefits: Quick thinking, as the leader role moves around the circle
Body awareness
Rhythmic speech coordinated with rhythmic motions

Comment: This short game is a good filler when the class must wait around a table for a few minutes.

Directions: Everyone slaps their thighs once on "Ali"
Everyone slaps their thighs again on "Baba"
Everyone claps their hands once on "Forty"
Everyone on "Thieves," the leader touches some part of his/her body such as the ears, eyes, neck, elbows, back, knees or toes and all the other children touch their own same body part(s).

After children learn the game, each child takes a turn leading the chant. The turn passes without breaking the rhythm.

Older children could think up more complex positions to assume on the word "thieves," such as placing one hand on the head, with the other hand pointing straight out.

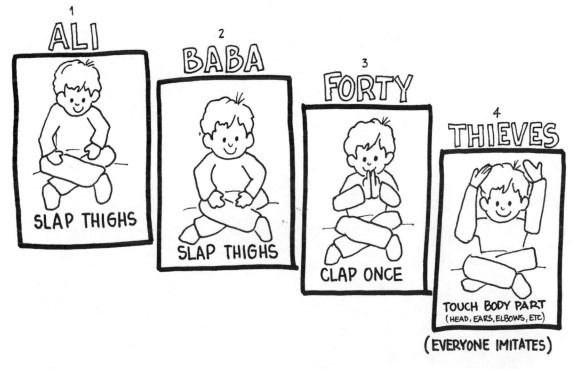

1 ALI — SLAP THIGHS
2 BABA — SLAP THIGHS
3 FORTY — CLAP ONCE
4 THIEVES — TOUCH BODY PART (HEAD, EARS, ELBOWS, ETC)
(EVERYONE IMITATES)

AUNT DINAH'S GONE
(A Chant)

Age: 2–6 years

Benefits: Development of a strong verbal rhythm
Children may take turns being the leader
Humor in assuming positions

Directions: The leader says a line and the group echoes it. In Verse 3, the leader assumes any "statue" pose, for example, arms up, arms out; one foot in the air; etc. The group then imitates the pose.

Leader: Aunt Dinah's gone!
Class: (echoes): Aunt Dinah's gone!

Leader: Aunt Dinah's gone!
Class: Aunt Dinah's gone.

Leader: Well, how did she leave?
Class: Well, how did she leave?

Leader: Oh, how did she leave?
Class: Oh, how did she leave?

Leader: Well, she left like this:
(leader assumes another pose)
Class: (imitates) Well, she left like this.

Leader: Oh, she left like this:
(leader assumes any pose)
Class: (imitates) Oh, she left like this.

All: She lives in the country,
Gonna move to town,
Gonna shake and shimmy
(everybody shake and shimmy)
Till the sun goes down.

(WELL, SHE LEFT LIKE THIS !)

Comments: This chant can be sandwiched in anywhere in the day, for example: after a transition, in the school van, or while waiting for lunch.

CRISS-CROSS APPLESAUCE

Age: 4–10 years

For: Sending and receiving nonverbal information
Eye-hand coordination ("drawing" an "invisible" pattern)
Tactile and kinesthetic awareness of shape and location
Following precise directions
Social skills (touching gently, having fun without silliness)

Directions: Try to work with a small group while learning the game (perhaps three or four couples). Have Children 1, 3, and 5 sit behind partners 2, 4, and 6. (See illustration.) The children in front are "chalkboards," and the children in back are "chalks." While saying the chant, children will draw with their fingers onto the backs of their partners, who are the "chalkboards" in front of them. After doing the chant and "drawing," the roles are reversed.

Verses:

Criss-cross, applesauce.	(Draw a big X, with a dot in the center.)
Spiders crawling up your spine.	(Tickle very lightly, upwards.)
Cool breeze.	(Children blow lightly on their partner's hair.)
Tight squeeze.	(Press the sides of the shoulders very gently.)
Now you've got the chillies.	(Tickle very lightly, downwards.)

Variations: Let the children experiment with "drawing" other letters.

Comments: Emphasize gentle and calm behavior so that the children can concentrate and visualize the patterns they feel.

THE FINGER BAND

Age: 2½–5 years

Benefits: Awareness of the order and sequence of ordinary events
Finger coordination
Language development in connecting words to gestures and actions

Directions and Verses:

1. Bring both hands from behind your back, opening and closing to the beat, while chanting:

    The finger band is coming to town,
    Coming to town, coming to town;
    The finger band is coming to town,
    Early in the morning.

2. Clap your hands on your knees to beat:

    This is the way they march and march,
    March and march, march and march;
    This is the way they march and march,
    Early in the morning.

3. Put your hands over your head, forming a point. Bob from side to side:

    This is the way they wear their hats,
    Wear their hats, wear their hats;
    This is the way they wear their hats,
    Early in the morning.

4. Clap your hands together in front of you:

    This is the way they play their drums,
    Play their drums, play their drums;
    This is the way they play their drums;
    Early in the morning.

Add other verses as desired, such as flutes, flags, guitars or horns.

5. Move your hands slowly behind your back:

    The finger band is going away,
    Going away, going away;
    The finger band is going away,
    So early in the morning.

6. Whispering

> The finger band has gone away,
> Gone away, gone away;
> The finger band has gone away,
> So early in the morning.

Variations:

Hallowe'en Version:

1. Old Mother Witch is coming to town, etc.
2. This is the way she rides her broom, etc.
3. This is the way she wears her hat, etc.
4. This is the way she scares you, etc.
5. Old Mother Witch is going away, etc.
6. Old Mother Witch has gone away.

Christmas Version:

1. Santa Claus is coming to town, etc.
2. This is the way he wears his hat, etc.
3. This is the way he drives his sleigh, etc.
4. This is the way he carries his pack, etc.
5. This is the way he places the gifts, etc.
6. Santa Claus is going away, etc.
7. Santa Claus has gone away.

Comments: Once "Finger Band" is well known, even three- and four-year-olds like to take a turn being the leader.

Bunnies can come to town at Easter time, Valentines can march into town on Valentine's Day.

FIVE LITTLE SOLDIERS
(Finger Play)

Age: 3–4 years

Benefits: Language development
Coordination of actions and words

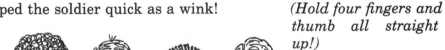

Rhyme: Five little soldiers standing in a row;
Four stood straight, and one stood so.
Along came the captain, and what do you think?
Up jumped the soldier quick as a wink!

1. Five little soldiers standing in a row: *(Hold hand with five fingers up.)*

2. Four stood straight, *(Hold hand with four fingers straight up and thumb relaxed.)*

3. And one stood so. *(Hold hand with four fingers straight up and thumb folded into palm.)*

4. Along came the captain, and what do you think? *(Move left hand along in front of right with index finger leading.)*

5. Up jumped the soldier quick as a wink! *(Hold four fingers and thumb all straight up!)*

Variations: Substitute different words for soldiers and the captain, such as "children" and "teacher"; "Indians"; "Chief" or "policemen" and "captain."

THE LITTLE RED BOX

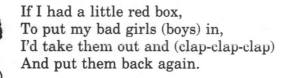

Age: 2–5 years

Benefits: Group togetherness with gentle humor and affection
Rhythmic speech and timing of the claps, kissing sounds and hugs
Practice of long yet easy sentences

Directions: The group chants together:

If I had my little red box,
To put my good girls (boys) in,
I'd take them out and (kiss-kiss-kiss sounds)
And put them back again.

If I had a little red box,
To put my bad girls (boys) in,
I'd take them out and (clap-clap-clap)
And put them back again.

If we had a big red box,
To put our good friends in,
We'd take them out and EVERYBODY HUG!
And put them back again.

Comments: The Little Red Box, with its gentle absurdities, reassures preschoolers that "good" and "bad" girls and boys are a universal phenomenon.

MISS SUE

Age: 4–7 years

For: Establishing a strong verbal rhythm
Matching words and motor actions
Socialization and humor
(Older children from 5–7 often establish intricate pat-a-cake patterns with a partner. Start with the Pease-Porridge-Hot pattern.)

Directions:

Miss *Sue*! *(Clap, clap)*
Miss *Sue*! *(Clap, clap)*
Miss *Sue* from *Al-a-bam-a*!
She's got A B C D E F G, *(Spin forefinger)*
She's gonna *play* some dirty tricks on me. *(Shake forefinger)*

She's got *smooth* skin *(Cross arms and stroke upper arms)*
She's got *smooth* skin *(Cross arms and stroke upper arms)*
She's got . . . *FREEZE*! *(Hold yourself "frozen" in any pose)*

Optional Insert: After "Alabama," add:
Say yes, say no, say maybe so,
Say, make a little motion *(Wiggle or dance)*

Comments: This little street game instantly captures children's imagination. Why? I'm guessing it's the strong rhythms, the nonsense and the faintly naughty, gossipy tone of the words. Who really knows? I have seen children repeat the chant over and over a dozen times or more. It usually becomes a girls' playground game. Who knows exactly why?

MOTHER'S KNIVES AND FORKS

Age: 2–4 years

Benefits: Language development
Coordination of actions and words

Rhyme: "Here are mother's knives and forks,
Here is mother's table,
Here is sister's looking glass,
Here is baby's cradle."

1. Here are mother's knives and forks, *(hands placed back-to-back)*

2.  Here is father's table.

3. Here is sister's looking glass,

4.  Here is baby's cradle.

Comments: Your grandmother probably knows this one! Very young children
can do this fingergame in a more simple way, without placing the
hands back-to-back, and without turning the hands "inside out."
Start with the hands palm to palm, with the fingers interlocked.

 EASIER "PALM-TO-PALM" BEGINNING

OH SAY, HAVE YOU HEARD ABOUT HARRY?

Age: 3–8 years

Benefits: Humor and fun with the several word meanings or puns
Coordination of actions with word signals
Body awareness

Directions: Children generally sit in a circle so they can watch each other (other children serve a mirror role). The children say the chant together, touching the various body parts as the words are spoken. The teacher should serve as a leader, and after the game is learned, children can take turns being the leader.

The Chant and Motions:

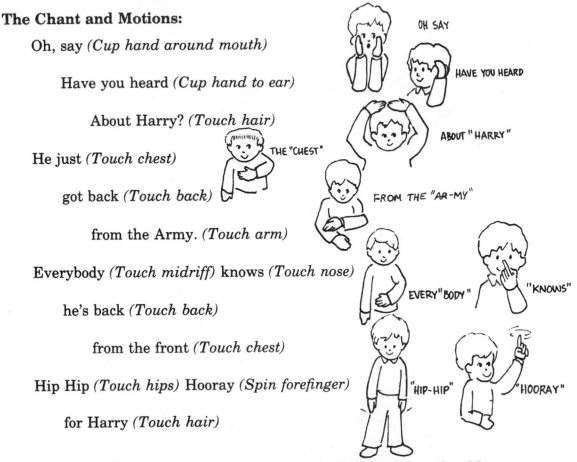

Oh, say *(Cup hand around mouth)*

Have you heard *(Cup hand to ear)*

About Harry? *(Touch hair)*

He just *(Touch chest)*

got back *(Touch back)*

from the Army. *(Touch arm)*

Everybody *(Touch midriff)* knows *(Touch nose)*

he's back *(Touch back)*

from the front *(Touch chest)*

Hip Hip *(Touch hips)* Hooray *(Spin forefinger)*

for Harry *(Touch hair)*

Comments: Even the youngest, most serious child gets the joke. Most young children require very broad humor, and this old-fashioned chant provides it. Understanding the humor of simple puns is a fine way to learn that language can be a source of great pleasure.

OLD MOTHER HOBBLE GOBBLE

Age: 3–5 years

For: Listening and echoing
Body awareness
Right and left awareness
Thinking up a stunt or motion
Speaking rhythmically with the group

Directions:

1. The teacher says a line, the children echo it.

Teacher:	Old Mother Hobble Gobble	Children echo:	Old mother Hobble-Gobble,
	Sent me to you,		Sent me to you,
	What can you do?		What can you do?
	What can you do?		What can you do?
	Shake your right hand,		Shake your right hand,
	Just as I do.		Just as I do.

2. Vary the verses any way, for example:

Tap your right foot, just as I do.

or

Scrape your left heel, just as I do.

or, getting more action into the game:

Hop all around, just as I do.

or

Jump up high, just as I do.

or

Run in place, just as I do.

or

Spin around, just as I do.

or

Rest awhile, just as I do.

"REST AWHILE—JUST AS I DO"

3. After children catch onto the chant, they can take turns being the leader(s).

ON MY HEAD
(Finger Play)

Age: 2, 3, and 4 years

Benefits: Language development
Coordination of actions and words
Body awareness

Rhyme:
On my head, my hands I place,
On my shoulders, on my face,
On my hips and at my side,
Then behind me they will hide.

I will hold them up so high . . .
Make my fingers quickly fly,
Hold them out in front of me,
Swiftly clap, 1-2-3.

Variation: When you know it well, say the whole rhyme in reverse, starting with "Swiftly clap, 1-2-3!"

Comments: This rhyme can be lengthened, or words and body parts can be changed. (Simply keep the key rhyming words intact.)

TWO LITTLE BIRDS
(Finger Play)

Age: 2 and 3 years

Benefits: Language development
Coordination of actions and words

Rhyme: Two little birds sat on a hill,
One named "Jack,"
And the other named "Jill."

Fly away, Jack,
Fly away, Jill,

Come back, Jack!
Come back, Jill!

1. Two little birds sat on a hill.

2. One named "Jack," *(wiggle Jack finger)*

3. And the other named "Jill." *(wiggle Jill finger)*

4. Fly away, Jack, *(throw Jack finger over shoulder)*

5. Fly away, Jill, *(throw Jill finger over shoulder)*

6. Come back, Jack!

7. Come back Jill!

Comments: The finger motions are only suggestions. You can certainly try out
some other ones.

Variation: Use as a play, with two children acting out the parts of Jack and
Jill.

PEANUT BUTTER AND JELLY

Age: Easy enough for 2½-year-olds, yet fun enough for 8-year-olds

Benefits: Coordination of movements and words or music
Organization and sequence of verses
Social skills such as humor and binding the group together

Directions: First the children should practice the movements that go along with the Chorus, as follows:

Children hold out both arms to the left and wave or "row" them to the music, like Hawaiian dancers. (See Illustration.) During this movement, they sing "Peanut! Peanut Butter," then whisper "and jelly!" as the arms are quickly shifted to the right side. (Directions are continued on the next page.)

After children master the little "Peanut, Peanut Butter and Jelly" Chorus, they are ready to *chant* the verses as follows:

1. First you have to pick it *(picking motions)*,   you pick it, you pick it,
                                                    pick it, pick it!

2. Then you crack it *(breaking motions)*,   you crack it, you crack it,
                                             crack it, crack it!

3. Then you mash it *(pounding motions)*,   you mash it, you mash it,
                                            mash it, mash it!

(Sing the Chorus twice.)

4. Then you stir it *(stirring motions)*,   you stir it, you stir it,
                                            stir it, stir it!

5. Then you spread it *(spreading motions)*,   you spread it, you spread it,
                                               you spread it, you spread it!

6. Then you eat it *(eating motions)*,   you eat it, you eat it,
                                         eat it, eat it!

7. Then you chew it *(exaggerated chewing motions)*,   you chew it,
                                                       you chew it,
                                                       chew it, chew it!

(Sing the Chorus again, twice.)

Comments: I have yet to see a child who didn't love this song. Try it and see for yourself.

TWO LITTLE APPLES

Age: 2–4 years

Benefits: Language development
            Coordination of actions and words

Rhyme: Two little apples hanging on a tree,
            Two little apples smiling at me,
            I shook that tree as hard as I could,
            Down came the apples, Mm! were they good!

Directions:

1. Two little apples hanging on a tree, *(Extend arms to side and cup each hand to make apples.)*

2. Two little apples smiling at me, *(Turn cupped hands forward.)*

3. I shook that tree as hard as I could! *(Shake body and arms.)*

4. Down came the apples, *(Squat down on ground.)*

Mm! . . . were they good! *(Rub tummy.)*

Comments: This activity is as old as the hills, but still fun!

Section B: Active Chants

The activities in this section are analogous to *Section I-B: Active Musical Games*. They share many of the same benefits found when children are using their entire bodies and moving freely about the room. Beyond that, active chants are often rich in body percussion; that is, in the various sounds that can be made with different parts of the body (clapping, snapping, patting, stamping, or clicking). Combine body percussion with movement and strong rhythm, and you have a winning combination.

Active games require both physical and mental discipline, but because the games are noncompetitive, novel and amusing, children gladly submit to the games' gentle rules.

CADENCE CHANT

Age: 6–8 years

Benefits: Practice in using the right and left feet
Movement to a definite beat
Development of quick reactions, i.e., thinking ahead for the step-skip-step at the end of the chant

Materials: A group of restless children, or the need to move a group from one place to another in a more interesting way.

Directions: Have children march, stamping the left foot as they walk; changing to stamping the right; and making a skip-change at the end of the verse. Then repeat all, emphasizing the left foot again.

FOOT: L R   L R   L   R   L   R

LEFT   LEFT   I LEFT MY WIFE IN TEN-NES-SEE WITH

L   R   L   R   L

FOR-TY KIDS AND A CAN OF BEANS AND I THOUGHT IT WAS

R   L   R   L   R   L   R L R

RIGHT   RIGHT   RIGHT FOR MY COUN-TRY WHOOP-DE-DOO
(STEP - SKIP - STEP)

Comments: A good mixer; a good way to get everyone's attention without "talking."

ANN
by Rita Shotwell
(Written for my friend Ann Geiler)

Age: 4 and up (this works better with older children)

Benefits: Auditory skills (responding to word cues)
Development of concentration skills
Use of body percussion
Coordination skills

Materials: None except for step 6, in which you need simple rhythm instruments

Directions: For young children, do all of this *slowly:*

1. Children sit on the floor, Indian style, in a circle. The teacher starts a steady beat by patting his/her thighs and having the children join in. The teacher says the chant through twice, while the children pat their thighs and listen to the words.

2. The teacher says one line at a time and the children echo them. (Stop patting thighs.)

3. The teacher again says one line at a time, which the children echo, only this time include two pats on the floor everytime you say the words, "Ann had," or "Ann gave."

4. Repeat again and *add* two pats on the thighs on the words "little red," "great big," "shiny black" and "quite a." (Do this in addition to patting floor.)

5. Repeat again and *add* two claps on the words "hat on," and "shoes on," with one finger snap on the words "bow" and "show."

6. If the children can handle all this, continue with the rhythm instruments:

   • Tone blocks, castanets and rhythm instruments: tap twice every time you say: "Ann had" and "Ann gave."
   • Maracas and shakers: two shakes every time you say "little red," "great big," "shiny black" and "quite a."
   • Bells: two shakes every time you say: "hat on" and "shoes on."
   • Finger cymbals and triangles: hit them once on the words: "bow" and "show."

Ann had a lit-tle red hat on,
Ann had a great big bow.
Ann had shi-ny black shoes on.
Ann gave quite a show!

CODE	BODY PERCUSSION	RHYTHM INSTRUMENTS
▬▬▬	STAMP OR PAT FLOOR	TONE BLOCKS CASTANETS RHYTHM STICKS
∿∿∿	PAT THIGHS	MARACAS SHAKERS
▭▭▭	CLAP	BELLS
✕	SNAP FINGERS	FINGER CYMBALS TRIANGLES

(I told the children to watch me closely, and whenever I hit the floor, the wood-sounding instruments would play. When I patted my thighs, the shakers would play. When I clapped, the bells would play, and when I snapped my fingers, the metal instruments would play. I went *very slowly*. This takes a lot of concentration for them.)

Comments: I did this activity with 4-year-olds in the Spring, some fourth through sixth graders and some senior citizens. It went over best with the older people. It was a very challenging activity for *all* the groups. With the older folks, we stood up and stepped up the pace. I was amazed that the fourth graders could handle it.

ANOTHER ST. PAT'S
by Bob Shotwell

Age: 3–6 years

Benefits: Auditory skills
Locomotor movement
Use of voice dynamics
Use of rhythm instruments

Materials: None except for part 5, for which you need simple rhythm instruments

Directions:

1. The children sit in a circle, while the teacher says the chant through once while class listens. Then the teacher says the chant, one line at a time, and the class echoes it.

2. Repeat the chant, only this time use voice dynamics:
   First line: whisper
   Second line: loud whisper
   Third line: a little louder
   Fourth line: shout
   (The teacher goes first and class echoes.)

3. Stand up and repeat the chant with the following movements:
   First line: jump twice
   Second line: march 3 steps (in place)
   Third line: step, slide to the right
   Fourth line: step, slide to the left

4. Same directions as Step 3, only *walk,* instead of *march* on Line 2. Keep moving around the room and step, slide instead of staying in place.

5. Add instruments:

    First line: play 2 beats on the tone blocks, castanets, rhythm sticks
    Second line: play 3 shakes on the maracas and shakers
    Third line: play 2 shakes on the bells
    Fourth line: play 2 taps on the finger cymbals and triangles

Chant:

Oh me! *(clap)* Oh my! *(clap)*
Would you look at that.
It's time again,
For another St. Pat's.

Comments: Simple enough for 3-year-olds, but can also be done with much older children. Have them suggest movements and instrumental accompaniment.

THE COOKIE JAR CHANT

Age: 5–10 years

Benefits: Development of rhythmic coordination
Feeling the beat and keeping the chant in rhythm while anticipating the next step.

Directions: Have the children sit in a circle and begin a simple clapping pattern. (The youngest children should begin by patting their knees, then progress to a "clap-pat-clap-pat," after they have learned the rhyme.)

All chant together:

GROUP : WHO STOLE THE COOKIES FROM THE COOKIE JAR?

TEACHER : ___NAME OF CHILD (IT)___ STOLE THE COOKIES FROM THE COOKIE JAR

CHILD (IT) : WHO ME?

GROUP : YES YOU!

CHILD (IT) : COULDN'T BE.

GROUP : THEN WHO?

NOW THE RHYME BEGINS AGAIN WITH THE CHILD WHO WAS "IT"
PICKING THE NEXT CHILD WHO IS "ACCUSED":

CHILD (IT) : ___(NAME)___ STOLE THE COOKIES FROM THE COOKIE JAR

With the younger children, it might be helpful for the teacher to chant *all* lines with the children until they have a solid feeling for the question and answer concept. At first there *will* be interruptions and pauses in the game, but this goal should be kept in mind: the rhyme should be chanted, passing from child to child without interruption as perpetual motion, until all children have had a turn to be named as the "thief."

Variations: The only variation to this game is the altering of the clapping pattern to make the game more difficult. The clapping patterns here are listed from easiest to hardest.

Step 1. Patting the knees *(in a steady beat)*

Step 2. Pat-clap-pat-clap

Step 3. Pat-clap-snap *(right)*-snap *(left)*

Step 4. Pat-clap-snap *(both hands together)*-clap

Comments: This game can be used effectively as a transition activity to dismiss children (one by one) to recess, lunch, bathroom or carpool. The bouncy rhythm is easier to catch onto if you remember there is a 1-beat rest or pause after Lines 1, 2, 6 and 7.

FIVE LITTLE BUNNIES
by Rita Shotwell

Age: 3–6 years

Benefits: Finger dexterity
Number recognition
Opportunity for dramatic play

Materials: None, except in Variation 1 (pictures of 5 bunnies)

Directions: The children sit in a circle. The teacher goes through the chant once while the children listen. Repeat the chant, one line at a time, using it as a fingerplay and have the children echo it. After the words, "along came the wind," pause and make the sound of the wind while moving one hand back and forth, pretending it is the wind trying to "knock down" the other hand. Say the chant 5 times, each time eliminating one bunny as the wind knocks it down. Use the appropriate number of fingers for the chant each time you start it again.

Chant: Five little bunnies went hopping into town,
Along came the wind (*pause for the sound of wind*) and knocked
     one down
"Oh my," said the rest, "we must do our best,
To keep from falling down!"

(Continue: 4 little bunnies, 3 etc., on 1 little bunny, "along came the wind and knocked him or her down and that is the end!")

Variations:

1. Make up a picture of 5 bunnies with a number on each one. Have the pictures duplicated so each child has one. Give each child a picture and a crayon, and have him or her cross off each number while saying the chant. Start with 5.

2. Select 5 children to be the bunnies. Everyone else will be the wind. The bunnies will hop "into town" and after "along came the wind," have the rest of the class start swaying their bodies back and forth and make the sound of the wind. One "bunny" will fall down and rest of "bunnies" and the teacher continue to say the chant, while the children make motions and the sound of wind. The bunnies will move like they are walking against the wind, having a hard time trying to stay up. Repeat 4 more times until all are "knocked down."

Comments: It was very interesting to watch the children with the bunny pictures and crayons. Some of the 3- and 4-year-olds had a little trouble finding the right number and crossing it out.

DOCTOR KNICKERBOCKER

Age: 5 years through elementary grades

Benefits: Attention-building
Development of the abilities to concentrate and think ahead
Practice in math skills
Body awareness

Directions: At random places in the room, but all facing the leader, have the children go through the chant 2 or 3 times, accompanied with a clap-pat pattern to get everyone to feel the rhythm of the chant. Then proceed as below with the actions added.

2. Now let's get the rhythm of our feet *(stamp, stamp)*
   Now we've got the rhythm of our feet *(stamp, stamp)*

3. Now let's get the rhythm of our hips *(whoo-ee!)* (swing hips from side to side)
   Now we've got the rhythm of our hips *(whoo-ee!)* (swing hips from side to side)

4. Now let's get the rhythm of our knees (knock, knock, bump knees etc.)

5. Now let's get the rhythm of our fingers (snap, snap etc.)

6. Now let's get the rhythm of our tongues (click, click etc.)

7. Now let's get the rhythm of our eyes (wink, wink etc.)

How many more movements can you think of?

Variation

1. For the children in the primary grades who have learned to count by 2's, 5's and 10's, another version of the chant is available. It can also be used with all the multiplication tables for the upper elementary grades:

    Directions: Get the children into a single circle, sitting or standing. Use a simple clap-pat pattern to keep the beat of the chant. The object of this game is to count by 2's, 5's or 10's in rhythm. You chant the introduction together, just as in the first version. The leader or teacher says the word "Go," and the child to his/her left begins by saying "two," followed by next child saying "four," then "six," etc., around the circle. Pick a number such as 100 at which to stop counting. If a child misses a beat or calls out a wrong number when it is his/her turn, he/she must pay a forfeit, go to the center of the circle and continue clapping the beat, until there are no people left in the outer circle. The leader begins the counting again after each mistake.

2. Name states, presidents, cars, trees or birds in rhythm.

Comments: The magic of the playground chant has been translated into a classroom activity.

COUNTING OUT RHYME
by Rita Shotwell

Age: All ages

Benefits: Exposure to counting "without numbers."

Directions: Children sit or stand in a circle. The teacher goes around the circle and says the rhyme, while tapping children lightly on the head or shoulder. Tap one child for each line. The last one tapped is the leader. (Continue repeating the rhyme if more than one child is needed.)

Rhyme: This one

That one

Let's pick

Just one

You

Are

It!

Comments: This is a good way to "choose" someone to be a game leader or to select several children for an activity. Picking a leader this way eliminates any problems with the unchosen children feeling "slighted." They can see that it was done fairly.

ENGINE, ENGINE

Age: 3–6 years

Benefits: Locomotor skills
Opportunity for imaginative play

Chant: Engine, Engine Number 9,
Running down Chicago line.
Running East, running West,
Running through the cuckoo's nest.

Directions: Say the chant through once while the children are standing in a circle. Have them move their bodies from side to side, while saying the chant.

Repeat, then have the children line up and hook elbows to make a "train." Move and say the chant.

Comments: Take your "train" to the zoo and have the children act out the animals they would see at the zoo. Children can guess what animal is being imitated. They could also act out eating food such as ice cream, hot dogs, etc. We have had a lot of fun with this activity!

GEORGY PORGY

Age: 4–6 years

Benefits: Use of voice dynamics *(loud and soft)*
Use of body percussion *(clapping, snapping fingers, etc.)*
Quick reactions and thinking ahead
Auditory skills *(listening and watching for signals)*

Materials: (Only on the Variation) simple rhythm or home-made instruments.

Directions: The children sit in circle with the teacher. The teacher says the chant one line at a time, and the children echo it.

Chant: Georgy Porgy pumpkin pie,
Kissed the girls and made them cry.
When the boys came out to play,
Georgy Porgy ran away.

Variations: Add voice dynamics with each line:

1. whisper
2. loud whisper
3. medium voice
4. shout

Add body percussion with each line:

1. snap fingers 4 times
2. clap 4 times
3. pat thighs 4 times
4. stamp feet 4 times

Add instruments for each line:

1. triangles and finger cymbals
2. bells
3. maracas
4. tone blocks and mallets

GHOST OF TOM

Age: 3–6 years

Benefits: Practice in following a simple sequence of directions
Use of vocal expression

Directions: The teacher will say the chant through once for the children while they are sitting in a circle. (Whisper to make it sound spooky.)

The teacher and children stoop down low in the circle. The teacher will say the chant one line at a time with movements *(see below),* and the children will echo the words and movement.

WOULDN'T IT BE CHILLY WITH NO SKIN ON?

Chant: Have you seen the Ghost of Tom?   (Rise up slowly to standing position.)
Long white bones with no skin on.   (Take 4 steps forward, bending over and moving your arms.)
Ooh, ooh, ooh, ooh   (Take 4 steps, making a small circle.)
Wouldn't it be chilly with no skin on?   (Go down slowly to a crouching position and hold your arms as if you're cold.)

Comments: You may know this as a song, but I found it to be more fun when chanted. The children become very quiet and wide-eyed.

HEAVEN CHANT

Age: 4–8 years

Benefits: Coordination of words and movement
Control of simple instruments to accompany the chant

Materials: For variation only: finger cymbals, triangles, tone blocks and mallets, maracas, sand blocks, tambourine, cymbal and mallet, or improvised instruments

Directions: Start in a large circle formation. Have the children say the chant and accompany it with movements. (Practice the movements and the chant separately before combining them.)

If you want to get to heaven let me tell you what to do:
(4 steps into circle)

Just grease your feet in mutton stew,
(make 2 circles with knees)

And slide right out of that slippery sand,
(step, slide twice)

And ooze on over to the Promised Land.
(turn around twice)

Yea!
(raise arms in the air)

Variation: Add instruments to accompany the chant and movement:

Line 1: Finger cymbals and triangles, 4 beats.
Line 2: Tone blocks and mallets, 4 beats.
Line 3: Maracas and sand blocks, 4 beats.
Line 4: Jingles and tambourine, 4 beats.
Line 5: Cymbal and mallet, 1 beat.

JACK BE NIMBLE

Age: 3–6 years

Benefits: Coordination skills
Development of concentration skills
Auditory skills

Directions: Say the chant while standing up and bending knees rhythmically. Repeat several times with a different direction each time:

1. Everyone stands in place to start. Jump on the word "jump."
2. Have the children pretend there is a puddle of water in front of them and on the word "jump," they are to jump over the puddle.
3. Have children walk freely around the room and jump on the word "jump."

Chant: Jack be nimble,
Jack be quick,
Jack jump over the candlestick.

Jump it lively,
Jump it quick,
But don't knock over
The candlestick.

Variation: Children can take turns walking and jumping one at a time.
Change "Jack" to the name of the child doing the movements.

Comments: This may be done at Halloween. Tell the children they are all going to be "Jack-o-Lanterns" when they say the chant.

I HAVE A CAT
(An Echoing Chant)

Age: 3–7 years

Benefits: Use of listening skills and memory
Development of physical and rhythmic co-ordination, imitation of
motions and chant

Materials: None; instruments can be used in Variation 1

Directions:

1. Ask children to listen and watch very carefully so that they can echo and mimic the story and actions as each line is spoken. After awhile they will know the story quite well.

2. Now tell them that you can "tell" the story without saying any words at all. The teacher will clap each line and the children will then tell the story in words.

3. Finally, have a completely "secret" story using no words at all. The teacher claps each phrase and the children clap back.

THE STORY: (CHANT SLOWLY)

I HAVE A CAT,
(CHILDREN ECHO & MIMIC)

THE CAT'S WHISKERS

MY CAT IS FAT.
(CHILDREN ECHO & MIMIC)

THE CAT'S "BELLY"

I HAVE A CAT,
(CHILDREN ECHO & MIMIC)

MY CAT WEARS A HAT.
(CHILDREN ECHO & MIMIC)

THE CAT'S HAT

I HAVE A CAT,
(CHILDREN ECHO & MIMIC)

MY CAT CAUGHT A BAT.
(CHILDREN ECHO & MIMIC)

"THE FLYING BAT"

I HAVE A CAT,
(CHILDREN ECHO & MIMIC)

MEOW!

Variations:

1. Use rhythm instruments to tell the story. (For example: a tambourine can be shaken each time the "cat" is mentioned.)

2. Have the kids be leaders. Be sure to echo whatever *they* make up.

Comments: This chant is a favorite of every child who is lucky enough to come into contact with it.

OOEY, GOOEY

Age: 3–10 years

Benefits: Auditory skills
Opportunity for imaginative play
Coordination of words and body sounds
Control of simple musical instruments

Materials: (For variations only) tone blocks and mallets, maracas, train whistle, hand drum and mallet or substitutes

Directions: All the children say the chant while up on their knees and moving their bodies and arms with a train-like motion. On "splat," fall down flat and then get up and say "Ooey, Gooey!" Can also have 2 groups: one "worms" and one "train" and act it out. On "Woo, Woo," pull your arm up and down to "blow the train whistle."

Chant: Ooey, Gooey was a worm,
Ooey, Gooey loved to squirm,
Ooey, Gooey on the track,
Woo, Woo—SPLAT—Ooey, Gooey!

Variation: Accompany chant with body percussion:
    2 stamps each time on "Ooey, Gooey"
    1 pat on the thighs on: "worm," "squirm," "track"
    Clap on "splat"
    Sound disgusted on last "Ooey, Gooey"

Add instruments:
    Use tone blocks each time on "Ooey, Gooey"
    Use maracas on: "worm," "squirm," "track"
    Train whistle on "Woo, Woo"
    Hand drum and mallet on "splat"
    (Children without instruments can use body percussion.)

Comments: Children love this chant!

NOBLE DUKE OF YORK
A Song for Younger Children

Age: 2–4 years

Benefits: Matching of actions to words; gives practice in acting out position words such as "up," "down," etc.
Listening skills for word-signals
Gentle humor

Directions: Children generally stand in a circle, but the song can be sung while they are seated in chairs. During the first line, "The Noble Duke of York," the children salute. During the second line, "He had ten thousand men," children march in place (if seated, they "march" with their hands on their thighs.)
Each time the word "up" is sung, the children stretch up tall.
Each time the word "down" is sung, the children stoop very low.
On the words "half-way," the children bend in the middle and make a sitting motion.

Variation: Sing the last line (or the whole song) quite fast, and see if the children can keep up with the motions.

Comments: This singing game is very popular with toddlers who think that changing quickly from up to down is great fun.

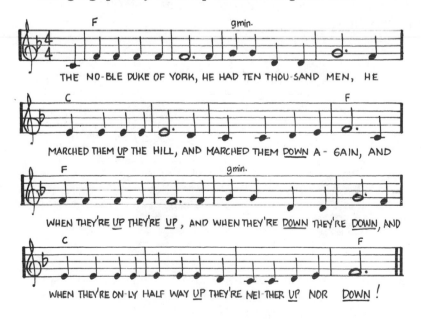

THE NO-BLE DUKE OF YORK, HE HAD TEN THOU-SAND MEN, HE

MARCHED THEM UP THE HILL, AND MARCHED THEM DOWN A - GAIN, AND

WHEN THEY'RE UP THEY'RE UP, AND WHEN THEY'RE DOWN THEY'RE DOWN, AND

WHEN THEY'RE ON-LY HALF WAY UP THEY'RE NEI-THER UP NOR DOWN!

PIGGLY-WIGGLY

Age: 2–5 years

Benefits: Humor and group fun
Match of very simple motions to words
Elementary "counting" on the fingers, without numbers
Auditory memory (remembering what comes next; anticipating the next line and its movements)

Directions: Children stand in a circle and "count" their fingers while saying:

This little piggy went to market (start with thumb);
This little piggy stayed home;
This little piggy had roast beef;
This little piggy had none;
This little piggy cried "Wee, wee, wee!" all the way home.

Now for the funny part: the children cup their hands around their mouths (as if shouting) and continue to chant:

He cried, "Oink! Oink!"   *(cup hands)*
Piggly! Wiggly!   *(wiggle hips and body)*
Oink! Oink!   *(cup hands)*
Piggly! Wiggly!   *(wiggle hips and body)*
Oink! Oink!   *(again cup hands)*
Piggly! Wiggly!   *(wiggle hips and body)*
All the way home.

Comments: This little chant draws a smile from the most sober child. True, it's educational value is minimal, but it puts everyone in a good mood, and that can be important.

ROSE, ROSE

Age: 3–8 years

Benefits: Use of voice dynamics
Coordination skills
Speech with movement

Directions: Children are scattered around the room, and say the chant several times using voice dynamics and movement to accompany the chant.

Chant: Rose, Rose, she has big toes,
She carries them wherever she goes!

Movements and Voice Dynamics: tip toe and use high voice;
bend down low and use a low voice;
stamp and shout;
take tiny steps and whisper;
run and chant fast;
take big steps and chant slow.

Comments: Children can also suggest ways of moving and changing their voices to fit the movements.

ST. PATRICK'S DAY CHANT
by Rita Shotwell

Age: 3–6 years

Benefits: Coordination skills
Auditory skills such as responding to word cues
Group cooperation

Materials: None except for the purpose of variety, through use of simple rhythm instruments

Chant: By gosh, by gum, by golly,
If it isn't St. Patrick's Day!
There's dancin', and laughin', and wearin' the green,
Oh my, what a happy scene!

Directions: The teacher says the chant through once while the children listen. Then he/she repeats the chant a few words at a time and the children echo them. Have 3 groups of children crouch down low. Then have them do the following:

Group 1. jump up and shout, "By gosh!" (remain standing)
2. jump up and shout, "By gum!" (remain standing)
3. jump up and shout, "By golly!" (remain standing)

All 3 groups jump up and down while saying: "If it isn't St. Patrick's Day!"

Everyone does a little dance while saying: "There's dancin',"
Everyone laughs while saying: "And laughin',"
Everyone struts around while saying: "And wearin' the green."

Continue to dance, laugh and strut for a minute or so after each line is said.

Everyone goes down slowly while saying: "Oh my, what a happy scene!" All jump up and shout: "Happy St. Patrick's Day!"

" THERE'S DANCIN',

AND LAUGHIN',

AND WEARING THE GREEN."

Variation: Use rhythm instruments. Form 4 groups of students with instruments sitting on the floor.

Group 1. castanets, rhythm sticks or tone blocks
      2. finger cymbals or triangles
      3. maracas or shakers
      4. bells

Group 1. play the instrument and say: "By gosh!"
      2. play the instrument and say: "By gum!"
      3. play the instrument and say: "By golly!"
      4. play the instrument and say: "If it isn't St. Patrick's Day!"

Group 1. play the instrument and say: "There's dancin',"
      2. play the instrument and say: "And laughin',"
      3. play the instrument and say: "And wearin' the green,"
      4. play the instrument and say: "Oh my, what a happy scene!"

Everyone plays and shouts: "Happy St. Patrick's Day"

Comments: Coordinating the instruments with words and different groups worked better with the older children. You may want to try just the movement with 3-year-olds.

TEDDY BEAR

Age: 2–5 years

For: Marching to rhythm
Acting out parts on the appropriate word signal
Listening and memory, such as anticipating what action comes next
Stopping and starting

Materials: None. However a string, rope or a circle taped on the floor helps small children stay in circle formation.

Directions: This chant is, of course, a well-known jump-rope rhyme. It can be used effectively as a march for children too young to jump rope.

Children stand in a circle (preferably a circle marked with tape or a rope laid on the floor. If a rope is used, the children march *outside* the rope, not on it.)

First practice all the motions (shining a shoe, turning around, etc.) while standing in place.

Next, while the teacher says the chant alone, the children walk around the circle, stopping to do the motions and then resuming the walk. Do not expect young children to march in exact rhythm.

Eventually, the children will be able to say the chant, march in some semblance of even rhythm, and do the motions.

TEDDY BEAR, TEDDY BEAR . . .

Verses:

1. Teddy Bear, Teddy Bear, turn around (children turn)
   Teddy Bear, Teddy Bear, touch the ground (children touch floor)
   Teddy Bear, Teddy Bear, shine your shoe (touch shoe)
   Teddy Bear, Teddy Bear, now, skidoo! (children jump)

2. Teddy Bear, Teddy Bear, go upstairs (children lift knees while
                                         stepping)
   Teddy Bear, Teddy Bear, say your prayers (children fold hands)
   Teddy Bear, Teddy Bear, turn out the light (pretend to pull a cord)
   Teddy Bear, Teddy Bear, now goodnight! (place folded hands under
                                            chin)

Variations:

1. Children could walk in a line around the room.
2. After children learn the game thoroughly, try speeding up the first verse, slowing down the second verse.

Comments:

This is probably the most widely-known jump-rope rhyme in the country. But it is probably brand new to most preschoolers.

If you're working with a large group of children, try dividing your group into two circles instead of one.

VALENTINE RHYTHMS
by Rita Shotwell

Age: 6 years and up

Benefits: Auditory skills
           Use of voice dynamics
           Use of body percussion
           Language skills: clapping the chant in syllables

Materials: None except for Variation 2 (simple rhythm instruments)

Directions:

1. Children sit in a circle. The teacher goes through the whole chant once while class listens. (Clap the rhythm of the words while saying them.)

    The teacher repeats one line at a time and the class echoes each one. Again, clap the rhythm of the words while saying them. If the children do not echo the line correctly, repeat it. They will have to listen carefully in order to echo correctly.

2. Repeat again, only this time use voice dynamics with the words. Have sound of the clapping correspond to the sound of your voice; for example, if you are whispering, clap softly. Whisper the first line, then whisper louder on the second line. The third line gets louder and fourth line is a shout.

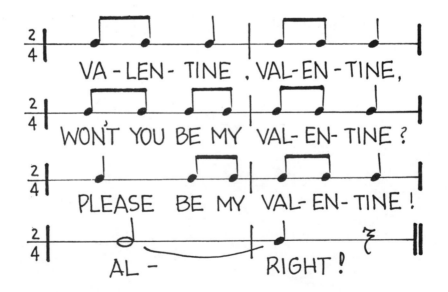

Variations:

1: Use body percussion with the chant: (Also speak words with body percussion)

First line: stamp the rhythm of words
Second line: pat your thighs with the rhythm of words
Third line: clap the rhythm of the words
Fourth line: snap your fingers with the rhythm of the words

Extend: Omit the words and use only body percussion. On the last line, smack your lips twice instead of snapping your fingers. (I didn't tell the children I would do this, so it came as a surprise "kiss"!)

2: Add the instruments:

First line: wood sounding instruments
Second line: shakers
Third line: bells
Fourth line: metal sounding instruments

Comments: I did not try this with 4- and 5-year-olds, but I feel that if you do this in the *Spring* and go slowly, they should be able to handle it. (I always say to try the harder activities with the younger children in the Spring because, by then, the children have had a year of training and they are almost a year older.)

SODA CHANT

Age: 4–8 years

Benefits: Auditory skills
Use of body percussion
Coordination of actions or sounds with words

Materials: None, except for rhythm instruments for the variation

Directions: Say the chant several times while the children stand in a circle. Each time, do a different action to accompany the chant, such as knee bends, patting the thighs, clapping hands.

Add movement: First line: walk 4 steps
Second line: fall down slowly
Third line: get up slowly
Last line: everyone "struts" around the room

" DR. PEPPER KNOCKED HIM DOWN "

Chant: Coca Cola went to town,
Dr. Pepper knocked him down.
Diet Pepsi picked him up,
Now they all drink Seven-Up!

Variation:

Add instruments: First line: tone blocks
Second line: bells
Third line: finger cymbals
Last line: all instruments

Comments: This chant always brings on a smile!

Part 3

GAMES FOR AUDITORY AND LISTENING SKILLS

All these activities could have been placed in one or more of the preceding categories (some are musical, some are chants, some are active, etc.), but all have special emphasis on unusual sounds or signals. They require extra care in listening or extra auditory awareness. Usually, the verbal content of the game is amusing and often surprising, so children do not perceive the extra effort they must put forth as a burden. Work and play are subtly combined, and everyone is a winner.

BEAR HUNT
(A Chanted Story)

Age: 3–8 years

Benefits: Practice in listening skills, sequencing concepts and use of memory
Development of rhythmic coordination

Directions: Instruct children to listen and watch carefully so that they can echo each phrase and imitate the motions as they accompany the story. Begin patting your hands on thighs to make a "foot-step" sound and create a beat; chant each phrase rhythmically, pausing to allow the children to echo them. Once you have found the bear, "run" back home (Rapidly pat thighs with hands).

Let's go on a Bear Hunt . . . (Echo)
We're going to find a Bear . . . (Echo)
Open the door, squeak . . . (Echo)
Walk down the walk . . . (Echo)
Open the gate, creak . . . (Echo)
Walk down the road . . . (Echo)
Coming to a wheat field . . . (Echo)
Can't go under it . . . (Echo)
Can't go over it . . . (Echo)
Have to walk through it . . . (Echo)
(Stop patting your thighs and rub your hands together to make a swishing sound.)

Got through the wheat field . . . (Echo)
Coming to a bridge . . . (Echo)
Can't go under it . . . (Echo)
Have to walk over it . . . (Echo)
(Stop patting your thighs and pound your fists on your chest.)
Over the bridge . . . (Echo)
Coming to a tree . . . (Echo)

Can't go under it . . . (Echo)
Can't go over it . . . (Echo)
We'll have to climb it . . . (Echo)
(Stop patting your thighs and place one fist on top of the other in a climbing motion.)
All the way to the top . . . (Echo)
(Salute and look from one side to the other.)

Do you see a bear. . . ? (Echo)

No (shaking head) . . . (Echo)

We'll have to climb down . . . (Echo)
(Place fist under fist to climb down.)

(Resume walking.)   Coming to a river . . . (Echo)

We can't go under it . . . (Echo)

We can't fly over it . . . (Echo)

We'll have to cross it . . . (Echo)

Let's get in the boat . . . (Echo)

And row, row, row
(All sing "Row, Row, Row Your Boat"
accompanied with a rowing motion.)

We got across the river . . . (Echo)

We're coming to a cave . . . (Echo)

We can't go under it . . . (Echo)

We can't go over it . . . (Echo)

We'll have to go in it . . . (Echo)

Let's tip-toe (Use fingertips to pat thighs.)

(Whispering):   It's dark inside . . . (Echo)

It's very dark inside . . . (Echo)

I can see two eyes . . . (Echo)

And a big furry body . . . (Echo)

(Yelling): It's a Bear . . . RUN . . . (Echo)

Patting your hands very quickly on your thighs,
run back to the river, row the boat across the
river, run to the tree, climb up and climb down,
run to the bridge and cross it, run through the
wheat field, run up the road, open the gate . . .
(it creaks), run up the walk, open the door . . .
(it squeaks), SLAM IT! (Clap hands together.)

Comments: This is one of the most loved chanting activities for children.
Young children are particularly fascinated with the story and will
request it again and again.

BEAN BAG GAME

Age: 3–8 years

Benefits: Auditory skills
Group cooperation
Development of quick reactions
Coordination skills
Development of concentration skills

Materials: Bean bag, triangle or other instrument, record with a steady beat, or a hand drum and mallet

Directions: Children pass the bean bag around the circle while the music is playing. When the teacher sounds the triangle, whoever has the bean bag passes it the opposite way. (Sound the triangle when the more alert children have the bean bag and then go to the slower ones. This will give the slower ones a chance to catch on to the directions so they won't "fluff up" immediately.)

Variation: Use a hand drum and mallet or tone block and mallet. The children pass the bean bag to the steady beat of the instrument; reverse directions when the triangle or different instrument is sounded.

Change your speed on the instrument: if you play quickly, the children pass the bean bag fast; if the teacher plays slowly, the children pass it slowly.

Comments: This was a fun activity for our Mother's Day Tea. The Mothers and children played the game together.

BOUNCING BUBBLES

Age: 3–6 years

Benefits: Provides experience in body control and estimating space, with emphasis on group cooperation and following the rules of the game

Materials: Some kind of equipment to provide musical background for "bouncing"! A phonograph and record do nicely, but a simple drumbeat also works well.

Directions: Have children stand at random in an open space. Using their hands they will smear imaginary soap film all around their body, then very carefully blow air from their mouths to make beautiful large bubbles that completely surround them. Once the bubbles have been formed, the children must be very careful not to touch the other children or furniture or else their imaginary bubble will *"POP!"* and they will have to sit down until they receive instructions to blow-up their bubbles again.

Using recorded music or a drumbeat, have the bubbles bounce around the room; watch carefully and strictly enforce the rule of sitting down if anything is touched. (The emphasis should be on controlling the body in space.) Change the pace of the bouncing from fast to slow, and try other movements like floating or spinning.

At several times during the activity, give the command: "1-2-3-POP." All the children should sit down (popping their bubbles). This gives the kids who have "popped," the chance to blow their bubbles up to rejoin the game.

As the children gain skill, the game can be made more challenging by making the "bouncing space" smaller and smaller, thus making it much more *difficult to* avoid contact.

Comments: This game is very popular and can easily be adjusted to be fun and challenging for different age groups. For 3- and 4-year-olds, it provides good opportunity to use positional vocabulary as they spread the imaginary soap film above their heads, under their feet, between their legs or behind their backs. If the younger children have a difficult time understanding exactly how delicate bubbles are, it might be fun to have some actual bubble experience. Add some soap to the water play or go outdoors and use some bubble soap to blow real bubbles.

HAPPY AND SAD FACES
by Rita Shotwell

Age: 3 through 6 years

Benefits: Response to visual clues
Awareness of emotions
Quick reactions, thinking ahead
Concentration skills

Materials: Two paper-plate hand-puppets. Take one plate and cut it in half, then staple it to the top of a whole one to make a pocket to put your hand in.

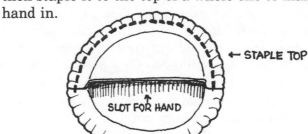

Draw a happy face on one and a sad face on the other.

Directions: Show the happy face; ask the children what kind of face it is, and then ask them to make happy faces themselves. Talk about things that make them happy. Do the same thing with a sad face.

Sing a familiar song such as "Twinkle, Twinkle" or "Mary Had a Little Lamb." Have children sing again, in either a happy or sad voice, depending on which face you hold up. (Sing the song all the way through in a happy voice, then again sadly, and finally, mix up the faces. The children can change their voices throughout the song, depending on which face you hold up.)

IF YOU'RE HAPPY

Age: 3–6 years

Benefits: Auditory skills (listening for sounds of instruments)
Concentration skills
Control of simple musical instruments
Quick reactions, thinking ahead

Materials: Simple rhythm band or homemade instruments

Directions:

1. Take the song, *If You're Happy and You Know It*, and change the words to: "If you're happy and you know it, play your instruments" (everyone plays).

2. Then change to individual commands: If you're happy and you know it, play the tone blocks (only that instrument plays). Continue with other instruments.

Comments: This activity helps the children learn the names of the different instruments, along with their sounds. Plus, the children have to pay attention because they don't know when their instrument will be called!

I recommend using at least 2 of each instrument. This gives children a sense of security, knowing someone else has an instrument like his or hers.

MISS MARY MACK

Age: 4–8 years

Benefits: Auditory skills
Practice in following a simple sequence of directions
Concentration skills
Coordination of actions with words

Materials: None except in the Variation. There, use simple rhythm or home-made instruments.

Directions: The children sit in a circle with you. Chant and clap on the repeated words at the end of each line. Chant again; omit the repeated words, but clap.

Chant: Miss Mary Mack, Mack, Mack,
All dressed in black, black, black.
With silver buttons, buttons, buttons,
All down her back, back, back.
She asked her mother, mother, mother,
For fifty cents, cents, cents,
To see the elephants, elephants, elephants,
Jump over the fence, fence, fence.
They jumped so high, high, high,
They reached the sky, sky, sky,
And they never came back, back, back,
'Til the fourth of July, July, July.

Variation: Pick 12 different instruments and have the children play when the words are repeated. The second time through, omit the words and only use the instruments.

Comments: With some older children, after the activity with clapping and instruments, I told them I had a special friend named "Mary Lou," and could they change the words of the rhyme to fit "Mary Lou"? The children changed all the lines except 5, 7 and 11. Try it; my students really had fun!

PEAS, PORRIDGE HOT

Age: 3–6 years

Benefits: Use of voice dynamics
Working with a partner
Use of body percussion
Quick reactions and thinking ahead
Concentration skills
Practice in following a leader

Directions: The children sit in circle with you. Use hand signals to indicate the voice dynamics:

when your hand is held high, they shout.
when your hand is held in middle, they speak in a normal tone.
when your hand is held low, they whisper.

The children say the rhyme. Keep changing your hand directions; the children follow with voice dynamics. The children can take turns being leader.

Chant: Peas, porridge hot,
Peas, porridge cold,
Peas, porridge in the pot,
Nine days old.

Some like it hot,
Some like it cold,
Some like it in the pot,
Nine days old.

Variation: Use "rotating" body percussion while saying the chant: (1) pat your thighs, (2) clap, (3) snap your fingers. (Use this same pattern throughout the chant.)

Chant and do body percussion with a partner: face your partner and say the chant. On the clap, clap hands with your partner.

Comments: When using body percussion with younger children, go slowly. They need time to get the actions coordinated!

PUSSY WILLOW

Age: 3–5 years

Benefits: Language concept: two meanings for "pussy"
Auditory discrimination: listening for stepwise progressions of sounds, both ascending and descending. This is a good tool with which to reinforce the high-low concepts.

Directions: Sing the song, making sure each new phrase is on a different step of the scale. On the word "scat," make the appropriate motion using both hands!

I HAVE A LITTLE PUSSY, HER COAT IS SOFT AND WARM, SHE LIVES OUT IN THE MEADOW,

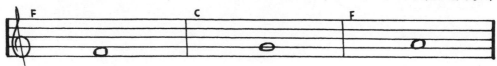

SHE'LL NEVER DO ME HARM, SHE'LL ALWAYS BE A PUSSY , SHE'LL NEVER BE A CAT,

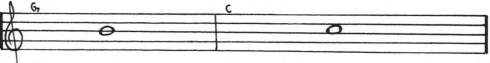

FOR SHE'S A PUSSY WILLOW   - NOW WHAT DO YOU THINK OF THAT ?!

MEOW, MEOW, MEOW, MEOW, MEOW, MEOW, MEOW, MEOW , SCAT !!!

Variations:

1: As you sing the song, use hand levels (low to high) to make a visual picture of the ascending melody. If you have a xylophone or glockenspiel, tip it on end and play the bars one at a time in an ascending pattern. Repeat the motions and/or instrumental accompaniment in the descending pattern with the "meows." Children can also use their whole bodies to show the ascending or descending movement of the melody by starting at a position close to the floor and stretching slowly to their limits. Reverse the positions for the descending melody.

2: This is a version of an old camp song using the same tune: a bit of humor is always in order!

Comments: The concepts of high and low sound are difficult for many children, and these songs present an enjoyable way to introduce the ideas.

RAINY DAY FUN

Age: 3 through elementary grades

Benefits: A lifesaver for "teacher"
Language development
Use of body percussion: snap, clap, pat and stamp
Control of simple instruments
Auditory discrimination: picking out the "teasing chant" on musical water glasses

Materials: Simple rhythm or percussion instruments (Example: drum, cymbals, sticks or castanets, finger cymbals, tambourines, triangles). Three water glasses, preferably all of the same size.

Variations:

Rainy Day Word Sounds—how many can you think of?

Drip, Drop, Pitter, Patter, Splish, Splash, etc.

Try chanting some of these sounds over and over, changing from one to the other to feel the different rhythm of the words:

Drip-Drop-Drip-Drop

Pitter Patter, Pitter Patter
Pitter Patter, Pitter Patter

Splish, Splash

Do it all together first, then divide the group and give each group a different sound. Do it in sequence and then simultaneously. Add some body sounds and build up a real rain storm.

Snap your fingers for the "Drip Drops."
Pat your thighs for the "Pitter Patter."
Continue to say "Splish Splash."

Add thunder and lightning by stamping your feet quickly, one after the other on the floor, and giving a mighty clap with both hands.

Leave out the words and try just the body sounds.

DRIP-DROP   PITTER-PATTER   SPLISH-SPLASH   THUNDER   LIGHTNING

Finally, transfer the body sounds to appropriate instruments:

Finger cymbals or triangles: Drip, Drop
Soft taps on sticks or castanets: Pitter, Patter
Shake the tambourines: Splish Splash
Drum roll: thunder
Crash on a large cymbal: lightning

Familiar Rain Chants:

RAIN RAIN, GO A-WAY.

LIT-TLE JOHN-NY WANTS TO PLAY.

IT'S RAIN-ING, IT'S POUR-ING, THE OLD MAN IS SNOR-ING, HE

WENT TO BED AND BUMPED HIS HEAD, COULDN'T GET UP 'TIL MOR-NING.

Set out 3 water glasses. Add water to each glass until you have matched the 3 tones in the "teasing chant." Try to play both of these chants on the water glasses.

TWO RAINY DAY SONGS

THE RAINDROPS FELL FROM THE SKY SO HIGH, PIT-TER PAT, PAT, PAT; PIT-TER PAT, PAT, PAT. THE

WIND BLEW THE CLOUDS A-CROSS THE SKY. PIT-TER PAT, PAT, PAT; PIT-TER PAT, PAT, PAT.

Directions: Holding their hands high above their heads, tell the children to let their fingers be raindrops. Tell them to take both arms and sweep them across the fronts of their bodies to "blow the clouds across the sky."

IT RAINED A MIST, IT RAINED A MIST, IT RAINED ALL O-VER THE

TOWN, TOWN, TOWN. IT RAINED ALL O-VER THE TOWN.

What else can it rain over? The school, the swings, the roof, the cars, the grass, the bus, me!

Comments: If you really feel ambitious, you can orchestrate all this rainy-day material into one big production. Older children could even suggest the format of this Rainy Day Dramatic Sound Piece!

MOVEMENT WITH COLORS

Age: 3–8 years

Benefits: Response to visual cues
Locomotor skills
Development of quick reactions (thinking ahead)
Coordination of sounds with movements

Materials: Colored construction paper

Directions: Show the children 4 pieces of construction paper, each a different color. Suggest different movements to the children, such as running, skipping, hopping, jumping, etc., then show the colors one at a time. Ask the children what kind of movement each color makes them feel like making (do this with each color). (Examples: green: running; yellow: walking; red: stopping; blue: jumping.)

Go over each color and corresponding movement, then hold the colors up and have the children react. As you change the color, they change the movement. The children can take turns being the leader and holding the colors.

Variations:

1. Instead of movements, have them suggest vocal sounds or add vocal sounds to movements such as: using a high voice with standing on tiptoe, or shouting with stamping.

2. Use rhythm instruments, assigning a different color to each instrument. With the instruments, you can hold up more than one color at a time because the children will have different instruments. You could also assign a color for a group of instruments such as: all wood sounds, all metal sounds, all bells, all shakers.

Comments: Children have to really concentrate on which movement or instrument goes with each color. You could make it more challenging by adding more colors.

RED AND WHITE (a chant)

by Rita Shotwell

Age: 3 through 6 years

Benefits: Coordination skills
Movement with words and rhythm
Color cues to learn left and right

Materials: Red and white crepe-paper streamers, red and white construction
paper cut into circles about 5″ in diameter, and masking tape.

$\frac{2}{4}$ 1 2 3 4

$\frac{2}{4}$ RED, WHITE. THESE ARE THE CO-LORS.

$\frac{2}{4}$ HERE'S RED, HERE'S WHITE. LEFT, RIGHT.

$\frac{2}{4}$ THESE ARE THE SIDES: HERE'S LEFT, HERE'S RIGHT.

$\frac{2}{4}$ RED, WHITE. MY SHOES ARE TIGHT.

$\frac{2}{4}$ LEFT, RIGHT. OH WHAT A SIGHT!

Directions: Put a red streamer on the left leg and a white streamer on right leg of each child. Use masking tape to put red and white circles on the floor and have the children stand on the circles, with the left foot on the red circle and the right foot on the white circle.

Say the chant and have the children march in place on the circles. Start slowly.

Start with the left foot and keep a steady marching beat. You will always end up on the red circle whenever you say "red" or "left," and on the white circle whenever you say "white" or "right."

Chant. 1 - 2 - 3 - 4
Red, white
These are the colors
Here's red, here's white.
Left, right
These are the sides
Here's left, here's right.
Red, white
My shoes are tight!
Left, right
Oh what a sight!

Variations:

1. For 3 year olds, you could make little red and white circles about 3″ in diameter and staple them to a popsicle stick. Give each child a red stick to put in his left hand and a white stick for his right hand. They can sit on the floor and, while you say the chant, they can alternate holding the sticks in the air.

2. When the older ones learn to march in place and keep the beat, then they can move on the circles (have circles set up in 2 lines or in a circle).

RESTING GAME
by Pat Stemmler

Age: 3–6 years

Benefits: Practice in listening and following directions
Exercise large muscles in a quiet controlled activity

Materials: A "quieter" rhythm instrument like triangle or finger cymbals

Directions: All children should find a spot where they can stretch out, lying flat on their backs. Be certain that there is plenty of room around them so that feet and arms can move without poking another child in the head. During the game, no one should speak except the instructor. When everyone is positioned and it's quiet, begin playing a very quiet beat on the triangle (or finger cymbals). Continue the beat for a minute or two, before giving the first directions:

Chant rhythmically and quietly:

Verses:

1: Lift one leg up in the air ... hold it up in the air ... now drop it! (If children are feeling the beat and all drop their legs at one time, they will hear a decided "thump." Then go on:)

Lift both legs up in the air ... hold them up in the air ... now drop them!

Lift one leg up in the air ... lift the other leg up in the air. Now lift both arms up in the air. Hold them up in the air ... now, drop them! (THUMP!)

(Continue the quiet beat on the triangle.)

(LIFTING . . . THEN . . . DROPPING)

2: Everyone close your eyes . . . now open them . . . close them, open them, close, open, close, open, close, open, close.

Repeat Verse 1.

3: Put one hand over your eyes . . .
Put the other on your tummy . . .
Now switch them, switch them . . .
(Speeding up:) switch them, switch, switch, switch, switch!

Repeat Verse 1 to conclude the game:

Add lifting their heads along with both arms and legs, and have them hold that position for several seconds before "dropping."

(SWITCHING HANDS FROM EYES TO TUMMY)

Comments: We invented this game one rainy day when the children seemed very restless, and it seems to have a wonderful, calming effect. It supplies equal amounts of relaxing and tensing of the muscles, and just enough silliness to bring on quiet giggles. Remember to chant quietly to create that "restful" atmosphere.

SOUNDS OF THE SEASONS

Age: 4–10 years

Benefits: Awareness of the sounds of nature, the city, or the country
Practice in following a conductor
Social skills (taking turns)
Communication in sounds

Materials: Poster paper (one large sheet), a marking pen

Directions: Talk about Spring or any one of the other seasons. Ask the children what sounds are common to that season and make pictures for those sounds on poster paper (divide the sheet into 6 or 8 sections and have one picture in each section). If you feel you are not capable of drawing the pictures, try to find pictures in magazines or the little books that would fit in with the season (perhaps the children could look through their magazines or books at home as a project for the class.

When the chart is finished, take a Spring Walk (or whatever season is chosen) and point to each picture. The children can then imitate the sounds they hear.

Use vocal sounds or simple instruments to imitate the sound of the picture. Example: finger cymbals could be used for the "sound" of snow falling.

Children could take turns being the conductor.

Examples:

Spring	*Summer*	*Autumn*	*Winter*
rain	crickets	cheers at	snow falling
birds	ocean	football	ice skating
sounds of	bouncing or	game	holiday
smelling	playing	leaves	sounds
flowers	ball	rustling	

Comments: I have found that any activity in which the children take turns being the conductor is a very good learning experience for them! The conductor has to watch the class and the class has to watch the conductor; there really has to be teamwork for such an activity!

STOP AND GO/FAST AND SLOW

Age: 3–6 years

Benefits: Development of auditory awareness such as following directions and listening for specific signals
Development of balance and coordination

Materials: One simple noisemaker for the teacher to use: a drum is ideal.

Directions:

1. Tell the group before you begin: "When you hear the beat of the drum, you may walk around the room. When the drum stops, you must 'freeze' wherever you are."

2. Play a simple beat on the drum and watch the children as they move around the room. When you stop beating, praise several of the children who remembered to freeze.

3. Begin the drum beat again and continue the game until the majority of children are able to STOP and GO on the appropriate signals. A little praise for good work really helps to focus the group on the task.

Variations:

1. *Fast and Slow:* Add the concept of moving quickly to a fast drumbeat and slowly to a slow drumbeat. It is still most important for the children to *freeze* when the drumbeat stops.

2. *High and Low:* Discuss the concepts of high and low with the children—can they reach high and squat down low?
   a. Using the drum again, establish two different sounds to use as signals for high and low, perhaps you could play on the rim or side of the drum. The clicking sound is very different from the resonant drumbeat—use it for the high movement. Use the regular drum for low.
   b. At this point many children will add ideas of their own: "Can we jump on high?" "Can we crawl on low?" Accept any appropriate suggestion with enthusiasm.
   c. Continue to remind to *freeze* when the beat stops.

3. *Kooky Beat:*
   a. Have the children think of bouncing, squirming and wriggling motions to make.
   b. Use the drum and rim to make a "Kooky Beat": not necessarily a rhythmic combination of sounds to accompany erratic, bouncing movement.
   c. Single out specific body parts to move: first the arm . . . then the leg . . . the head . . . and the eyeballs. Have the children move those parts while they hold everything else still.

SIREN STORY

Age: 3–6 years

Benefits: Response to a visual cue
Concentration skills
Following simple directions
Awareness of high and low sounds

Materials: A short story about a fire engine, a picture of a fire engine siren (I cut mine out of a story book about a fire engine). Paste the picture on 8½ × 11″ poster paper.

Directions: Show the siren picture to the children and have them make the sound of a siren. When they make the sound, have them hold out their hands (palms up) and move them up as the sound goes up and (palms down) down as the sound gets lower.

Tell the children you are going to read a story about a fire truck. Each time you hold up the picture of the siren, they are to make the sound and use their hands and arms to accompany the sound. (Make little marks in the story where you want to interject the siren sound.)

Comments: The siren picture gives the children a visual cue. It is also necessary to watch the teacher carefully. Because children are motivated, this activity is a good attention-builder.

TWINKLE, TWINKLE, LITTLE STAR

Age: 3–6 years

Benefits: Awareness of emotions
Language development of words and their opposites

Directions: Sing the song, *Twinkle, Twinkle, Little Star*. When you are finished, tell the children to sing the song again, only this time sing, as though you are very sad and crying. (Someone invariably will start to laugh before we are finished and I immediately say: "That's just what we are going to do next. The opposite of sad is happy, so we are going to sing the song again as though we are very happy.)

Sing very, very quickly; then very slowly.

Sing with a very high voice; then a low voice.

Comments: All the children who have tried this activity have had a lot of fun!

WHO HAS A RED DRESS?

Age: 3–5 years

Benefits: Language development
Social awareness

Directions: Sing the above question, and the individual wearing the red dress should sing this answer:

> I have a red dress, red dress, red dress,
> I have a red dress all day long.

> or

The whole group sings the name of the person wearing the red dress:

> Jeanie has a red dress, red dress, red dress,
> Jeanie has a red dress all day long.

Question: Who has a zipper on his jacket, zipper on his jacket, etc.
Answer: Johnny has a zipper on his jacket, zipper on his jacket, etc.

Instead of dealing with colors and clothes, you might sing about lost teeth, new baby sisters, special show-and-tells or any "happening." You might think of things the whole group has in common!

Variation: The tune lends itself to many situations. Use it for transitions from one activity to another, such as:

> Let's pick up our toys now, toys now, toys now,
> Let's pick up our toys now and get ready to eat.

> or

> Let's pick up our toys now, toys now, toys now,
> Let's pick up our toys now, one, two, three.

> or

> Tiptoe to your mats now, mats now, mats now,
> Tiptoe to your mats, sh-sh-sh.

Comments: The question and answer format individualizes the activity. You can make this tune sound like a march, a waltz, a trot or a lullaby. Try it!

VOCAL PUNCTUATION

Age: 4–10 years

Benefits: Ability to match sounds with visual cue
Concentration skills
Development of language skills

Materials: Make up 4 charts, 8½×11″. Put one punctuation mark on each chart: a comma, a period, an exclamation point, and a question mark.

Directions: Make up a sound for each punctuation mark, then read the story and hold up the card for punctuation and have children sound it out.

Story: Hey you, come here.
I said, come here!
What do you think you're doing?
You're doing what?
I don't believe this!
Do you know what he just told me?
Guess.
No, you're wrong.
Guess again.
You're right! That's it!

Variation: (For older children) After this has been done, you can divide the class into groups and give them 5 minutes to come up with an ending to the story (What was the child doing?).

Another day, you can have groups each make up their own story with punctuation sounds and have them perform for each other.